Hannah's Daughters

Hannah's Daughters

Six Generations of an American Family

1876-1976

Dorothy Gallagher

Thomas Y. Crowell Company
Established 1834
New York

Library of Congress Cataloging in Publication Data
Gallagher, Dorothy
    Hannah's daughters.

    1. Women—Washington (State)—Biography.
1. Title.
HQ1412.G34   301.41'2'0922   75-38557
ISBN 0-690-01103-2

1 2 3 4 5 6 7 8 9 10   Designed by Lynn Braswell

Contents

Introduction

In August 1973, I was asked, by a national magazine, to go to the state of Washington to interview Hannah Lambertson Nesbitt and her descendants. I did, knowing about them only the remarkable fact that they were a family of six living matrilineal generations, the first of them a woman of ninety-seven, the last a child of two. Through this family the magazine hoped to document the ways in which the lives of women have changed, have, from mother to daughter, become visibly freer, more open to possibilities. I spent very little time with the family on that first visit, a total of perhaps seven hours. Even so, I came back to New York with the premise of the article demolished. Whatever else the passage of almost a hundred years had accomplished, it had not brought those particular changes.

In February of 1974 and again in August of that year, I went back to Washington. This book is the result of conversations with each member of the family over a period of six weeks. Because they are women and there have been so many changes in surnames, when I refer to the family collectively I will call them the Lambertsons— Hannah's maiden name and the way she has begun to think of herself again. None of the names used are the real family names.

I said that this book is the result of conversations. They were not conversations in the sense that there was an equal exchange of information. I asked questions. Of Hannah, it was difficult to ask very detailed questions, since she is almost deaf and cannot see well enough to read. But she lives so much in her memories and is so starved for company that my presence was enough to turn her thoughts into speech. On some days she seemed able to hear better than on other days, and then, with the right pitch of voice and volume, I could say, "Tell me more about that," or, "What happened during the war?" or, "How did you feel about it?" Mostly I listened. With the others—her daughter May; Grace, May's daughter; Barbara, Grace's daughter; and Lisa, Barbara's daughter—I would also have preferred to be a passive listener so that my own biases would not intrude. But this wasn't possible. May and Grace are very private people, reluctant to talk about personal experiences and feelings. "When those things happened, I tried not to think about them," May said to a question about her first marriage. And that has been her style, as it is her daughter's. They have a distaste for looking too deeply into things, and an ethic of not "peddling" their troubles. Still, with my urging, I think they said more than they realized, and this makes me a little uneasy.

Why should any of them have talked to me about their lives, told me things they sometimes felt were shameful and that they have not said even to one another? I tried to explain why I felt that their story was important.

Hannah's ancestors migrated to America from Holland in the middle of the seventeenth century. Now, more than three hundred years removed from the direct cultural influence of Europe, the Lambertson women have lived as pure an American experience as there is. And if the kinds of lives people live have a great deal to do with the society in which they live, then the lives of these women have much to tell us about our world and about the actual experiences of people, particularly women, in it.

I don't mean to suggest that the Lambertsons are a typical family. They are their

own women, not cardboard illustrations of a point. But in some general ways they are more like than unlike most Americans. No member of Hannah's line of the family has been educated beyond high school, and the three older women did not finish high school. None has much money, and Hannah barely has enough for subsistence. They are not the hard-core poor but the working and lower middle class, and their lives have centered on making enough money to get by. The fathers and husbands of the Lambertson women have been farmers, loggers, itinerant laborers, small shopkeepers; the women have done everything from farm work to bookkeeping. In the sense that none of them has erupted into history, they are ordinary women. Their generations have lived through the changes from an agricultural to an industrial world; through wars from those with the Indians to the one with the Vietnamese; through a series of economic depressions and the great farm, labor and political movements of social discontent. In none of these public ferments have they participated directly, although of course they have taken the consequences. No one knows better than Hannah, for instance, what industrialization did to the life of the independent farmer. But, for the most part, the Lambertson women have taken the world as they found it, accepting it at its own evaluation, proud of their self-reliance and willingness to work. Paradoxically, despite their acceptance of the moral injunction to work hard, their expectations of reward have been very modest. They know that no matter how hard they work, they will never be rich, that this is a country where "money talks" and that they will never have enough of it for their voices to be heard.

As with most of us, the discontent they have felt has been focused on their personal lives. Things went wrong, but it wasn't always clear what, or why.

I came to the Lambertsons from another kind of experience—as a first-generation American, born of parents who made the migration in search of opportunity, intellectual and political opportunity as well as economic. Obviously I had certain biases. I assumed, for one thing, that all parents had aspirations for their children beyond what they, themselves, had accomplished. I thought, too, that if any people were candidates for the labor struggles of the early twentieth century, it would be the Lambertsons. And I assumed that until fairly recently, marriage had been, if nothing else, a stable institution.

None of these assumptions was borne out.

Lambertson mothers did not urge their daughters toward education or even toward advantageous marriage. As for the labor struggles, "The men in our family never had anything to do with unions," Grace said of her father and grandfather. And marriages among the Lambertsons failed in the first four generations—a rate much higher than the statistical average—but even in 1890, about the time Hannah's first marriage dissolved, there were already almost 34,000 reported divorces in the United States.

Beginning with Hannah, who, as she says, took "a step down" with her first marriage, the Lambertson family has remained socially and economically static, generation after generation.

This acceptance of things as they were puzzled me. Wasn't America the country where the possibility of progress was the justification for all hardship? Where I would have expected a crying out against fate, or a placing of blame on the established order, there was a resigned stoicism. In time I came to understand something about it. In order to advise a child to do differently, one must have a sense of one's power to affect the course of life; and, more than that, some sort of experience that offers a vision of life's larger possibilities. To have joined in the early union struggles—a dangerous act in those days—was dissonant with the ideal of independence, was for a man to diminish his pride, to admit he couldn't make his way by himself. And, not incidentally, to put at risk the life that was already pared close to the bone, the job that was already marginal.

How and why people change what they believe is a complex question. But, in part, it has to do with being directly touched by the powerful currents of other ideas. The Lambertsons have lived in a kind of social isolation, moving among people who lived as they lived, knew what they knew, believed as they believed.

Even had they wished to defy custom or authority, there was never much time to think about it. The immediate always pressed: food, clothing, shelter. There was never a time when they could rest from providing these necessities. "The children had to eat."

The nature of the work the Lambertson women have done has changed over the generations. The years that Hannah remembers as her happiest are those when she was an integral part of a family farm, each member with a variety of jobs to do, each making a visible contribution to the welfare and independence of the family. But when the farm was gone she "worked out," doing what she had once done for her own for every "Tom, Dick and Harry," and her descendants have taken their places in the industrial system.

Marriage has been no haven for the Lambertson women. Husbands deserted, or were thrown out when they became too brutal or refused to fulfill their responsibilities as providers. And this happened time and time again. More often than not, the women were the sole support of their children. The illusions and hopes of marriages entered into by inexperienced young girls were shattered early, and not without great cost to the women and their children.

Unlike characters in a novel, there are few clarifying turning points in these lives. Except perhaps for Barbara, introspection is a way of thinking they have neither learned nor felt able to afford, for questioning can undermine the foundations of a whole life. The Lambertson lives have moved on in some inexorable logic, each event making the next seem inevitable, each generation beginning again at the beginning, groping along an already well-worn path. The outsider provided with this aerial view may see external forces at work, but the women, immersed in the details and crises of their own lives, are like soldiers reading a report of the battle from which they have emerged battered but alive. The whole grand scheme has little to do with the chaos, the noises, the silences, the flashes of light and dark which were their experience.

Now, having distanced myself from the Lambertson women, I want to say how close I do feel. I have come to think of them as *my* family. Not only because their lives have been my work for more than a year, but because their lives are different in degree, perhaps, but not in kind from my own and from the lives of others I know. If the Lambertsons so often seem victims of a world they never made, so are we all to the extent that we are unaware of the social, economic and psychological forces that order our lives.

In a more personal sense, I know more of the Lambertsons' history than I do of my own family's, and I have a stronger sense of their continuity. Hannah is present for

William & Nell
Lambertson &
Hannah: 1876

me as the young girl she was, as vividly as is the ancient woman I met. She has made her times, her relatives, even the friends she mentions once and never again, whole and real. She has the gift of storytelling; her words make pictures. If because of their habit of caution and reticence I did not come to feel as close to May or to Grace as I would have liked, I did become close to Barbara, with whom I share a generation. Barbara, too, felt it was important not to clothe what actually happened with pride or illusion, and she told family secrets it may distress her mother to realize her daughter knows. Daughters always know more than mothers think they do; and they have a particular view of the woman whose part in their lives has been so important.

There are some difficulties with life stories told in retrospect. One is that many of the everyday things that mitigate life—the pleasure of conversations, laughter, visits—are lost in the telling, so that only the highest and lowest points stand out. And another is that the teller sometimes cannot recall what was known and felt at the moment, the past always being changed by the present. These are not problems I have tried to overcome. To have done so, I felt, would impose my idea of authenticity on things I could not know. So I have asked as many questions as I could think of and then let the Lambertsons speak for themselves. The rhythm and construction of language is their own. I have taken the stories, which came to me in bits and pieces, and given them the form which I felt expressed them best.

Hannah

William Lambertson ———— Eleanor Ogden

Earl Barlow ———— Hannah   Nicholas

May   Charles

Hannah: 1974

Oh, it was all so long ago. Everything's happened between now and then. *Everything's* happened. Nellie Dawson and her sister Lottie, gone this long time. All those I worked for, those I nursed and those I scrubbed their floors, dead these many, many years. And their children gone too. I'm left alone.

The last time I saw Hannah Lambertson Nesbitt was late summer of 1974. The foothills of the Cascade Mountains, which surround the Yakima valley, were baked dry and brown, most of the rain caught by the Cascades to the west. Out in Fruitvale, where Hannah lived, the streets were deserted in the heat except for a lone cat, squatting in the center of one of the roads that stretch in all directions into the hills. This fruit- and hops-growing valley was irrigated out of volcanic ash at the end of the nineteenth century. More than seventy-five years have not been enough to root its settlements in the landscape. Against the sculpted hills all signs of human habitation look shabby and transitory.

Hannah was ninety-eight that summer, and she no longer left her house. Her sight was failing; she could see only shapes and the difference between light and dark; and she was almost deaf. Walking had become a slow, painful process. She lived alone in a rented gray-asbestos-shingled bungalow of three small rooms. In one corner of her front room was a television set, which she could no longer watch; in the middle of the long wall stood a brown metal oil furnace; under one of the two windows a sewing machine table held two scraggly plants; and under the second window stood an oilcloth-covered table on which she put things when she wanted to remember where they were. There were also two vinyl-covered chairs in the room, and a rocking chair, in which she slept at night because age had humped her back and it hurt too much for her to lie down. Jerry, her Manx cat, was chained to a desk on the far wall so she would always know where he was.

Except for the times I visited her, when there was no stopping the flow of words, Hannah's days go like this: She wakes at six in the morning, pushes herself out of the rocking chair and goes to her kitchen at the back of the house. She cooks one third of a cup of minute oats; if she has a banana, she adds that to the cereal and sprinkles it with brown sugar. She eats her breakfast from a folding metal tray-table in the kitchen. When she finishes she washes the pot and bowl. She washes them slowly, more slowly than she has to, because it is work and work is precious and fills the time.

Then she shuffles back to one of her vinyl chairs and sits there, head sunk on her chest, dozing, until she is hungry again. At noon she cuts two slices of white store-bought bread and spreads them with softened margarine. Until the spring of 1974 she made her own bread. I watched her one day early in March, kneading the dough at the oilcloth-covered table, her head bound in a dish towel so no stray hair would fall into the dough. It was snowing that day, and the white snow-reflected light from the window etched each line dark into her skin. By the beginning of summer, she was no longer able to bake.

All through the afternoon Hannah sits in her chair. She daydreams, sometimes she sleeps; the distinction between the two is no longer important to her. At six o'clock she eats white bread again; sometimes she fries potatoes in Crisco and makes a potato sandwich. She washes the dishes, and then she calls her daughter-in-law. She makes this call night and morning, to let someone know that she is still alive. Sometime during the evening she moves from the vinyl chair to the rocking chair, covers herself with a blanket and goes to sleep. At four in the morning, which she says is when the weather changes, she wakes, finds her way to the toilet and then goes back to sleep two hours longer.

So it is, six days a week. On Sunday her son, Charles, and his wife, Ruby, come to eat Sunday dinner. Until a short while ago Hannah and Ruby took turns cooking Sunday dinner. When it was Hannah's turn, she fried chicken and made bread and apple pie. Now she has stopped cooking, but on the Sunday that is her turn she gives Ruby the money to buy a Kentucky Fried Chicken dinner, so it is still her dinner. She eats greedily on Sundays, getting all the comfort that food eaten in company can offer. Then, Sunday is over and the week begins again. One day during it a letter will come from her daughter; on another day her granddaughter may write. Once a month a check comes from welfare.

Hannah Lambertson was born on July 11, 1876, in Hope Township, Barry County, Michigan. The year she was born General Custer was killed at the Battle of Little Big Horn. Charles Lambertson, Hannah's uncle, was one of Custer's scouts. The history of the Lambertson family is a long one, traced back almost a thousand years. Only the barest facts are recorded, but they are more than enough to connect the Lambertsons with history; and they give a perspective to the lives of Hannah and the daughters who descend from her.

Nine centuries ago Hannah's ancestors came as conquering Norsemen to the coast of France and left descendants there who eventually migrated to Holland. In 1390 a Wilhehus Lambertsen was Burgomaster of Amsterdam. When the Spanish Inquisition came to Holland, the Lambertsens joined William, Prince of Orange, in the long war to drive the Catholic Spaniards out. The Lambertsens' coat of arms tells the story of their role in that war: a withered uprooted tree, symbolizing near extermination of the family; battle-axes of combat; and a swan, crowing and flapping its wings in final victory.

In 1646 two Lambertsen brothers, Joris and Pieter, migrated to America and settled around what is now Brooklyn, New York. On May 14, 1663, Joris married Jannetje de Rapelje in the Dutch Protestant Reformed Church of Brooklyn. So began Hannah's line in America.

The Lambertsen brothers had come to the New World as gentlemen, and they quickly acquired property. They prospered and multiplied. Jannetje bore eleven children, and most of them had ten, eleven, even twelve more. They made advantageous marriages. In the second generation, Laurens, the eldest son of Joris, married a widow named Hannah Dey, who already had three children, as well as a five-acre farm that ran from what is now Broadway in New York to the edge of the Hudson River. "Dey Street" still marks the road that ran through the middle of her farm. Later, in 1708, Laurens bought 5,500 acres of land from the Indians in what was the wilderness of

New Jersey. Not surprisingly, he became a rich farmer and was appointed one of His Majesty's judges from New Jersey.

Mary Lambertson, born in New York in 1699, married a John Reading, who became one of New Jersey's provincial governors. And their daughter Ann married into the family of George Clinton, governor of New York and, later, vice president of the new United States.

The Revolutionary War found the Lambertsons divided. By then they were in their third generation in America, and most had done well under British rule. Laurens' son Joris became a lieutenant in the British Army. Johannis Lambertson was a known British sympathizer; his property was confiscated, and he fled to Nova Scotia. Jacobus Lambertson was imprisoned for the same reason, but he managed to escape and join the Loyalist forces, for which the British rewarded him, after the war, with 3,000 acres in New Brunswick.

Thomas Lambertson, on the other hand, was one of the heroes of the Revolutionary Army. He fought with General Montgomery at the siege of Quebec, was taken prisoner there by the Hessians in 1776 and sent to the Jersey prison ships. In 1790 he was elected to the Pennsylvania legislature.

Toward the end of the eighteenth century, Lambertsons began to push the frontier west. A later Johannis moved to Ohio to farm; Richard Allen, who lost, through fire, the saw and flouring mills he had inherited from his grandfather, moved to farm in Iowa. His daughter, Annette, graduated from the Women's Medical College of the University of Chicago in 1881 and became the first woman member of the Nebraska Medical Society. Charles, Hannah's uncle, the Indian fighter and scout for Custer, lived to become the governor of Lower California and the owner there of vast tracts of land.

Some Lambertsons abandoned farming for business. In the early nineteenth century, Richard was a real estate operator on Long Island, buying large tracts of land, subdividing and reselling them at a good profit. He was also treasurer of Sussex County for twenty-six years and president of the Sussex Bank.

At least two Lambertsons are known to have fought in the Civil War. Asa, an adventurous man who made the long journey around Cape Horn to California, returned East to enlist in the Union Army. He served two years and died of fever in an Army hospital. John Lambertson was one of the 20,000 wounded at Antietam, the bloodiest battle of the Civil War.

The opportunities of industrialization were not lost on the Lambertsons. Arthur Lambertson, born in 1813 in Pennsylvania and educated by the practical Quakers, was one of the founders of the Elgin Watchworks in Chicago. Beekman Van Buren Lambertson, born in 1809, is said to have invented both the diving bell and the centrifugal mill. But no other Lambertson did as well as Hannah's great-uncle William.

William was born in New Jersey in 1818. When he was sixteen he left home to set himself up as a fur trader in Michigan. He traded successfully with the Indians and married an Indian woman, a fact that the records mention discreetly: "First [married] when quite a young man located far from civilization in the forests of Michigan." Jane, the daughter of this marriage, was sent to be educated in Switzerland. What happened to William's Indian wife is not recorded, but he married twice more, gave up fur trading for the more lucrative lumber business and bought a small mill in Muskegon. This he replaced with a larger mill, and in 1851 he moved to Chicago to run his business from there. When his grandson, Hannah's second cousin, died in Chicago in 1952, he left a fortune of five million dollars, plus a collection of paintings bequeathed to the Art Institute of Chicago. Just so close was Hannah to a life of wealth, travel, culture and a luxurious old age.

The success of Hannah's great-uncle William brought other members of the family to Michigan—his younger brother Nicholas and Cornelius, their father. Nicholas arrived in the 1840s with his wife, Sarah, and established himself as a fruit farmer. He and Sarah had six children. William, their second from youngest child, was born in Michigan in 1857. On July 5, 1875, William married Eleanor Ogden, the daughter of an English family that had migrated first to Canada and then to Michigan. The July following their marriage Eleanor, who was called Nell, gave birth to Hannah. The July after that, Nell bore Nicholas. On the second of January, 1879, Nell died of pneumonia. She was not yet twenty years old.

Hannah: 1876-1893

Sometime in the late summer or early fall of 1876, William and Nell took their infant daughter to a photographer's studio. Hannah, wearing a white christening dress, lay sleeping on her mother's lap. Nell was eighteen, a plump girl with a square face, blue eyes and light hair. She held her daughter stiffly, and her expression is a little sullen. William stood behind his wife and daughter in the conventional pose, one hand resting lightly on Nell's shoulder, the other dangling from his waistcoat pocket. He was only twenty-two, already a righteous and responsible family man.

In this last quarter of the nineteenth century, the Lambertsons, like more than seventy percent of the fifty million Americans, lived on a farm. The farm was still the ideal way of life: America was to be a nation of farmers, each self-sufficient and independent, their labor given dignity by the ownership of their land, "each man working for himself among his equals," as Crèvecour wrote in the 1780s.

The Homestead Act of 1862 was to be the legal expression of this ideal. Not only would it give all those who worked the land valid title to it, it would also ensure lack of conflict between labor and capital in the eastern states, which were becoming rapidly industrialized. Those in the cities who could not find work or who were dissatisfied with their wages would have the alternative of going west and living by their own labor.

But between 1862 and 1890, while the population of the West increased by more than ten million, only two million were able to claim title to the 160 acres promised by the act. Two hundred million acres were owned by the railroads; more belonged to speculators. The abundant free land was for sale, and the farmer, in many cases already a tenant, found himself dependent for his living on factors outside his labor: on the railroads to which he paid ruinous freight rates; on absentee landlords to whom he paid high rents; on the banks to which he mortgaged his farm to buy new steam-driven equipment.

"We are not only putting large bodies of our new lands in the hands of the few," wrote Henry George in 1871, "but we are doing our best to keep them there. . . . To say that the land of a country shall be owned by a small class is to say that that class shall rule it . . . that the people of a country shall consist of the very rich and the very poor, is to say that republicanism is impossible. . . ."

The year 1873 began a long period of depression. In the cities, three million people were unemployed; even if they had the skills to farm, they had no money to transport themselves and their families west, to buy the land that was no longer free and to wait until a crop could be raised. There was violent labor trouble in the cities, and the depression devastated the farm economy.

Hannah, at the age of three, was living on her grandfather's farm—prosperous apple orchards unaffected by the depression. But her father, William, had given up farming. After Nell's death he had become a logger, working in the north Michigan woods, leaving Hannah with his parents, and Nicholas, her brother, boarding with strangers. The elder Lambertsons lived in the southern part of Michigan; the farm was called Orchard Place, about ten miles from the nearest town of Hastings. Apart from the apple orchard that produced the farm's main crop, other fields were planted with wheat, and there was a large vegetable garden for the needs of the family and the hired help. Hannah's grandfather also raised hogs for the market, and there were the other usual farm animals—cows, chickens, workhorses.

There were three houses on the Lambertson land: a small log cabin in which tenants lived, a larger house on the far side of forty acres of uncleared woods, where the hired men slept, and the main house itself. This was large and luxurious for a farm-house. In the parlor the black walnut sofas and chairs were hand-carved with bunches of grapes and upholstered in velvet. They had been a gift from Hannah's great-uncle William on his brother's marriage. But Nicholas Lambertson was a moderately wealthy man in his own right, and everything in the house was the best money could buy. The tableware, from teaspoons to soup ladles, were sterling silver; the dishes were bone china; the glasses, cutware. Hannah's clothes were made for her by a dressmaker who came to the house; another seamstress came to make the linens and do the mending. There were so many in hired help that two sittings were needed at mealtimes and the big dining-room table was completely filled at each. Two or three times a year visitors, with names like Tiffany and Wanamaker, came by railroad from the East, bringing their own servants with them.

This was the setting in which Hannah was raised. Her earliest memories are frag-mented, but she is old enough now so that the past is more vivid than the present.

She begins with an incantation:

·   ·   ·

I was born in Hope Township, Barry County, Michigan, on July the eleventh in seventy-six. And I lost my mother the second of January in seventy-nine. Left me three years old, my brother a baby.

Oh [she says, sitting in her small gray house, almost a century later]. Oh, it was all so long ago. Everything's happened between now and then. *Everything's* happened. Nellie Dawson and her sister Lottie, gone this long time. All those I worked for, those I nursed and those I scrubbed their floors, dead these many, many years. And their children gone too. I'm left alone.

A song comes to her mind:

Where's that baby's mother?
In the baggage coach ahead . . .

She vaguely remembers a train, noisy and jolting through the countryside. There is a baby on the train, and it screams at the top of its lungs. A woman takes the baby in her arms and it quiets. In the baggage coach ahead is a coffin; her father sits beside it, holding his head in his hands.

She remembers another coffin; someone holds her up to see the body inside. She recognizes the woman who lies there. Once she saw that woman standing at a table, a dish of eggs beside her. It is her mother's mother.

A year or two later she remembers a stranger looking at her. "Whose kid is that?" She listens for the answer. "Oh, that's William's brat."

A hired girl sings to her:

> *You're always in the way*
> *You're always in the way*
> *You can't go out and play*
> *Your own mamma would even say*
> *You're always in the way*

From the time she was about five years old she remembers exactly how it was.

My grandaddy had an awful big farm. There were about forty acres of woods and I roamed right through it. I used to spend my time in the woods and eat all the wild stuff I could find. I always knew when the sassafras bark was tender to eat. I was always watching for the beech leaves to chew them. Eating. I was always eating. I knew when the wintergreen was coming up, because I watched for the berries. And the mandrake! Grandma told me one time. She says, "When the mandrake comes up with just two leaves on it, that's the male." I didn't know what a male was, but I knew it didn't have any apples on it. But then the other would come up and it would have a little curl on it and a big cream-colored blossom. That was the female and it had the apples. I could smell the mandrake just as far as they could be, and I got the first ones every time. I'd get an apronful of them and go along and eat them.

I could run around the woods all I wanted, but my grandmother was elderly and I might as well have been in a convent. I wasn't allowed to whistle. Oh, I wanted to whistle so bad. I had two cousins, Abe and Kate, and they were beautiful whistlers. If I had any envy at all it was that I could whistle their tunes. But Grandma wouldn't allow me. She wouldn't allow me to climb. The only thing I could do was get something to stand on and reach up as far as I could. And I wasn't allowed to laugh. I could smile but not laugh. And I had to keep out of the lake. My dad was a figure skater, but Grandma wouldn't allow me on the ice at all. Never had any dolls to play with. I used to play with praying mantises and frogs and toads and lizards. Those were my playmates.

Hannah's grandmother was born Sarah Gordon in New York State about 1820. She survived the cholera epidemic of 1832 which spread through the Northeast and South, killing thousands. Both her parents died in the epidemic. A few years later Sarah married the brother of her sister's husband, went west with him and bore six children, five boys and a girl. Apparently she wanted no more children to raise, since Hannah's brother was boarded out. Perhaps because Hannah was a girl, her grandmother saw her as a duty that could not be refused.

Sarah was a formidable looking woman: Black & Clarkson's, photographers of Jefferson Street in Hastings, Michigan, took a portrait of a woman in her sixties, hair pulled back tightly behind large ears and fastened at the crown. Her nose is Roman, her mouth small. Two deep lines on either side of her mouth, like those on a ventrilo-

Sarah Lambertson
(Hannah's
grandmother): ca. 1880

quist's dummy, separate her chin from the rest of her face. Her eyes stare straight ahead in disapproval.

Oh, my grandma was good to me, if leaving a kid to wander alone all over the place is good. I had the very best of clothing, the very best of eats. But no love, and that's what I wanted. If they loved me, they didn't let me know it. Oh, my daddy loved me, but I didn't see him. Not once a year hardly. He was always in the north woods, working. He was a river driver, you know, and he worked up there with the French people and learned their language.

You know, the logs are cut in the woods and dumped in the dam in the river. And then the river drivers ride them down to where they're sold, in Chicago and places like that. You have to ride those logs and keep them in line with the current. Dad rode them down the Manistee River, from up north near Kalkaska, way down to Lake Michigan. He had special boots for it, with a fringe sticking out on the sides. And he had a peevy to keep the logs together. You had to know your job to be a river driver. You can get crushed if the logs jam up. And if you fall in between them you can drown. And when you get in the rapids it's pretty dangerous. Dad had to do that because he had my brother to support. Of course you didn't get much in those days—sometimes not over ten dollars a month. But you had your bed and you had your meals.

Sometimes Dad would bring my brother home to visit and he would sleep in my room. I slept in a bedroom off the dining room. Sometimes there was a hired girl in there with me, but most of the time I had the big bed all to myself. When my brother would come, Grandma would bring out the trundle bed for him. She wouldn't let him sleep in the bed with me. Oh, she was so afraid he'd wet her bed! He was awful fragile, Nick was, he was a sickly baby, living hither and yon. Oh, he was a blessed brother. There were just the two of us.

I don't know, but I was *told* that my mother dearly loved her children. My mother must have meant an awful lot to me. I don't remember her, but when I went to bed I used to play I was dead, so I must have known something. And I think I remember something my mother taught me. Every time we had thunder I'd lie in my bed and try to figure out what God was saying. Now where *did* I get that notion? I must have been taught that before I can remember. I believe it was my mother who taught it to me. I might have been afraid of the thunder one time, and my mother might have held me in her arms and told me that story.

Oh, if there had been a hired girl who liked children, things might have been different with me. But it didn't work out that way. My grandma had more servants than she had children. I don't know how many she did have. I didn't know enough to count in those days. Grandma always called them "the girls." Of course they all had their own names, but when she talked about them she'd say "the girls." And she always thought about them. She said they had enough to do without shining the silverware, so she'd do that herself. And she said they had enough to wash and iron without the napkins. And Grandma'd get all of her bread and all of her pastry ready herself. She'd go into a room even the hired girls didn't go in, and she'd get her bread and pastry ready and carry it out and put it in the oven. Nobody went in that room but Grandma.

Grandad had his hired labor. I'd eat with them, with the hired men. There was an awful big table with a drop leaf down to the floor, and I sat on one end—there was a place just for me—and Grandad sat at the other end. When the men was done, the table was cleared off and reset, and Grandma would sit down to eat with the girls. She said if they was good enough to work for her they was good enough to eat with. I don't *know* why I didn't eat with the girls. Maybe there wasn't room for me. But the men was all nice to me. When they was done eating, they filed outside to smoke or chew or whatever they done, and have a chat. I'd go out with them. I can just see them chewing their tobacco and spitting out the juice. I'd go and get my cornsilk and have a chew with them.

The men all liked to eat at the Lambertsons'. They always got all the ham they wanted. Everywhere else they worked they only got chicken or beef. But we had a big smokehouse. In winter, when breakup was, Grandma had the hired help cut up all the meat in the smokehouse and slice it. Then she'd put it on the stove so it got hot. Not cooked, but hot all the way through. They'd put that down in big crocks covered completely over with lard. And they'd put those crocks in the basement. Come threshing time, they'd get the crocks up and cook the meat. That's what they fed their threshers. Smoked ham. They all liked it. They liked the way the Lambertsons ate.

In my grandaddy's time it was different than it is now. It was all hand labor, and men could support their families. Now, I don't know how other people were, but my grandaddy always saw his men had a good place to sleep and that their clothes were washed and mended. We had poorhouses, yes. A lot of men lived on a poor farm. I used to know a portion of a song about a son who persuaded his parents to deed him their farm. Well, they yielded to him and he turned them out. They had to go "over the hills to the poorhouse." That's what the song was called. There's many children did that to their folks. But I'm talking about what *my* folks done. They looked after those that needed help. If a man took sick or died, they looked after his family. Grandaddy sent Grandma to different places; she had several families she used to keep. She'd clothe them and everything else. She'd just go to visit and see what they had to have. Not insulting them, just bringing it out in the conversation. And if they needed a barrel of flour, they got it. And if their woodpile was getting low, in the morning they'd find a woodpile. My folks never thought anything of it. It wasn't advertised. It wasn't bragged about. The farmers just did it. They helped those that needed it. Not like it is today. Grandma took me on visits to her families, so I learned how that was done.

And I had to learn how all the stitches were made. Grandma was very strict. Every stitch had to be just right. I never learned how to sew, because we had our own dressmaker. Never learned any domestic sewing, because we had a woman come to the house to make our sheets and pillowcases. I learned all the stitches, but I never learned how to make anything. I tried to make doll dresses, but I didn't have the doll. In those days women wore hoop skirts and they wore bustles. My, a dress looks pretty when it's

Hannah:
1876-1893

31

draped over a bustle. Daytimes, around the home, the women wore small hoops. But when they'd dress up to go anywhere, they wore bigger ones. I was just a kid, so I didn't have a hoop, but I used to make believe. I'd drape material over my finger the way the big folks wore their bustles. I'll tell you what I wanted: I was so entranced by the work our dressmaker turned out I told Grandma, "Grandma, I want to be a dressmaker." Oh no, *I* couldn't be a dressmaker. I was a *Lambertson!* So I thought if I couldn't be a dressmaker I'd be a milliner. Grandma came down hard on that too. Oh, I wish I'd had some knowledge.

Grandaddy taught me some things. He got me a little slate, and I'd sit on the top step and he'd teach me the letters and how to cipher. I didn't care so much about the letters, but I did like to figure. And I did like to read. I don't know what books I read. I guess I read the Bible more than anything. I did have a temper when I was a kid. I was quick to snap. Grandma showed me in the Bible that when Jesus was angry he opened not his mouth, he said not a word. So I learned to say one, two, three, four, five, six, seven, eight, nine, ten, until I'd conquered myself.

My folks were Methodists. I went to church when I couldn't get halfway to the floor with my feet. My feet was just sticking straight out. And I had to be so still. I sat next to Grandma and if I wasn't still I'd get that *look* from her.

Oh, my! Grandma was strict. She taught me never to touch what belonged to anyone else. Once there was a hired girl sleeping in my room, and she had some writing paper and what they call indelible pencils. You wet them with your tongue and they make an awful pretty purple mark. Well, I don't know how many sheets of that girl's writing paper I destroyed. I was having lots of fun with her pencils. Then, after, I went out visiting. There was a point in the road that went to Hastings, and some people name Pratt lived there. I was sitting on their fence, swinging my legs and talking away when Grandma called me. Well, you know what I got? I got tied to the bedpost in Grandma's room. I had to drink a big glass of milk because the lead in those pencils is poison and the milk kills it. And I had to stay tied to the bedpost until bedtime, when I went to bed without my supper. I never touched that hired girl's writing paper anymore. But, oh, those were awful pretty marks I made. I left them all laid out there for anyone to see.

I'll tell you another thing about how my grandma taught me. Now, when I was young my hair was yellow. Yaller. I had so much hair, so long, so thick. Oh, what hair I had! I used to wear it put up with a circular comb, and I was always breaking my comb. Well, Grandma had just got me a new one, and she said that if I broke it she wouldn't get me any more; she'd have all my hair cut off. Well, one day I was standing at the sink and there was some dough on a rolling board right next to me. I don't know what got into me. I took my comb off, put it on the rolling board and went *thump!* Just like that. Broke it. Next day I had to go to the barber shop in Hastings and have all my hair cut. That barber had an awful time. It hurt that man to cut my hair. He cut it all off, just like a boy's, and I think he got a good price for it. When I got to school the children said, "Why, Hannah! What happened to your *hair?*" I didn't have so many friends after that. When my hair started to grow in, it came in red. Not a fire red, just a red tinge. But Grandma had to keep her word, didn't she?

She taught me not to snoop either. I never snooped but once. I don't know how old I was, ten, eleven, and I'd been teasing her for a ring. Grandma made all kinds of excuses about why she couldn't buy me a ring, but I got it in my head that she'd bought me one for Christmas. And I hunted all around the house until I found it. It spoiled my Christmas for me. I did *not* enjoy my Christmas. I betrayed my grandmother's faith in me. I never snooped again.

Oh, I learned to be boss of this creature! I learned to be good. And if I didn't bother anyone, they'd let me stay around when the big folks talked and I'd hear a lot of stories.

Now, when I was a little kid I used to hear Grandma say, "I wonder whatever happened to Charles." Uncle Charles was my grandfather's brother. Older than him. He was married to Clara Clayborn and they had two little girls. She was going to have another baby, when Uncle Charles went away to war. I don't know what war that was but, anyhow, his wife lost track of him. Letters were carried by pony mail in those days and they got lost. Well, this is what I heard happened. Uncle Charles was in San Francisco, but nobody knew that. One day when he was an old man he picked up the paper and read something about a Governor Charles Lambertson of Lower California. Well, Charles Lambertson was *his* name too, and it was a family name. So he went down there to Lower California and looked up this Governor. The Governor was rich. He owned 70,000 acres of land, and he thought that some old codger had got hold of a family history and was trying to get someone to take care of him in his old age. So he sent a telegram to Uncle William, Grandaddy's other brother. Uncle William took the first train out there. As soon as he seen the old man, he knew it was his own brother that he'd been wondering about for the last forty years. And this man who was the governor was his brother's son, the baby that hadn't yet been born when he left home. Uncle William took Uncle Charles back east to York State, and he spent his last days with his daughter Clara.

He'd had two daughters, you know. I heard tell that his other daughter, Rachel, started out for California by covered wagon with her husband and her mother-in-law. She was never heard from again. Now, I heard it said that her husband might have killed her. It ain't fitting to say that, but I heard Uncle Charles tell that story. Now, whether her husband killed her or whether the Indians got her, we don't know. Indians would do that in those days, you know. But I think it was her husband that killed her because she never got on with her mother-in-law.

The Indians we had back in Michigan would never hurt anyone. Oh, we had some beautiful Indians. My millionaire Uncle William had a wife who was a chief's daughter. A princess. You know, the Sioux can walk through a forest of twigs and you'd never hear a sound. My grandad had a friend who was a Sioux chief. He and a bunch of his friends would come to the farm to visit. They'd put their teepees up and spend the summer there. They had one little boy, same age as I, all dressed up in buckskins. He was dressed just like his daddy—buckskin suit, and that headgear hanging clear down to the ground. We'd play some Indian game—I don't know what it was. Trotting around, just trotting around. It was some game they had.

Is this the first day of March? My, what a snow! Come in like a lion, it'll go out like a lamb. Of course it ain't too cold, because the flakes are large. If you're from back east you know that when the snow comes down soft and hangs on the branches, it's a short stay for that snow. I learned that back east. Of course Michigan ain't as far east as York State. That's what my folks called it. They never said *New* York or *New* Jersey. I've never been in York State, but that's where my grandma was born. I heard her tell how her people died when she was quite young. There was an epidemic of cholera and her folks died all in the same week. Whatever room a sick person died in, they were carried out the window. They weren't taken through the rest of the house where the well people were. And they had so many to bury that week, they didn't bury them very deep. There was one young woman buried, and the next day she came walking home. That dirt had drawed the cholera right out of her.

I had a schoolmate, Lizzie Rourke, and she had what they now call TB. We called it consumption. Well, her mother took her to a lake, and every night Lizzie buried herself in the mud. In the mornings she'd jump in the lake and wash off. She cured herself. The dirt pulled the consumption right out of her. We knew all those things then.

I remember one time I went huckleberrying with my Aunt Laura. We went into the marsh where the berries grow high. And my dog Rover came with us. Well, a rattlesnake bit Rover on the nose. Aunt Laura made me go home and I had an awful time because Rover didn't follow us. "Oh dear me suz, Rover's going to die!" How I bellyached because Rover was out in the woods dying. I just mourned for him. And in two days Rover came home well, with the mud packed dry around his nose. That animal knew enough to go and hunt for some good mud and get his nose into it.

Now another time I was looking at Charlie Mixer. He was an elderly man and, oh, he was a statuesque man. Tall. Straight. He was wearing some spectacles and I was looking at him because there wasn't no glass in them. Grandma wore glasses, so I knew what they were. Well, Grandma thought I was looking at Charlie Mixer's nose and she gave me a twist on the arm. I didn't know it, but he had a false nose made from a mold, out of wax. And the spectacles were to hold the nose on. He'd had cancer, you see, but he'd cured himself with red clover blossom tea.

I wish I'd known those things when my mother was sick. She'd been ill and the pneumonia set in. I could have cured her. What you do is you get a lard pail and fill it full of water and put some vinegar in it. And when it comes to a boil you throw a blanket over the patient so they don't have anything to breathe but what comes off that water. I could have cured my mother. I know I could of. But it didn't happen that way. She died. Everybody's dead, aren't they? Grandad died when I was about eight years old. We left the farm right away. Grandaddy left it in his will that Grandma was to keep the farm or sell it if she wanted to. She sold it and we went to Hastings, went to town to live. Oh, I hated to leave the farm. I knew every foot of those woods.

Grandma bought property in town and had a house built for her and Uncle Ben. He was her favorite child. You know what he was called by all the hired help on the farm? A snake in the grass! Didn't they like *him?* In later years I heard Grandma wasn't happy. I don't think her daughter-in-law was nice to her. That house had all Grandma's furniture and silverware and chinaware, but Grandma had to pay her board, and hire to have her washing and ironing done.

37

No, she wasn't happy. Not any happier than I am. She died two or three years before I came out West. There wasn't anything the matter with her; she just willed herself dead. You can do that, you know.

When we moved to Hastings I had to do housework there because after Grandma sold the farm, she just had one girl to do the general housework. So she put me to washing dishes. I was so small I had to stand on a box to do them. Grandma showed me how to scrub them, and I always washed them that way ever since.

In my growing years I was in the city. I went to the town school. Darned if I know how old I was when I left school. Ninth grade when I left, so I guess I was about fifteen. I was sick all the time in those days. Nobody knew what was the matter with me. That's when I learned how to crochet. When I'd get tired of crocheting I'd ask Grandma if I could go visiting, and I'd go see another old lady. Every old lady was Grandma to me. I was brought up to love old people. I had lots of grandmas. I'd go visit and read to them and talk to them. I'd never visit my schoolmates. I couldn't bear to go there, because they had their mothers to hug them, you see, and I couldn't stand to see that. Because I never had that.

I lived with my grandma until I made a fool of myself and got married. I thought it was all right to marry. I thought I'd have someone to care for me. They don't care as much as you think they do. William's brat's had a lonely life. A lonely life. I've had this awful feeling in here ever since my mother died. Nothing ever satisfied that. My daddy, my brother, my own children. Nobody ever touched that feeling. That hurt was always there. But, anyhow, I got by.

Hannah: 1893-1898

In 1893, Hannah married Earl Barlow. She was seventeen years old. In a photograph taken just after her marriage, her face is a slim oval, framed by hair swept back in wings. A gold watch is pinned to the bosom of a high-necked black silk dress, and it is easy to imagine that, past the edge of the photograph, the dress shows off a tiny waist. Hannah looks into an unfocused middle distance with what may be the beginning of a smile, a very pretty, gentle-looking girl who knows how to make fine stitches but not to sew, to wash dishes but not to cook, to carry out the obligations of a lady to the poor but not to be poor.

The depression that began in 1873 continued with intermissions until it turned into the great depression of 1893. In 1894, Jacob Coxey, of Ohio, organized some of the unemployed for a march to Washington to demand relief through public works. But the President, Grover Cleveland, had the members of Coxey's Army arrested for trespassing. When the Pullman Company drastically cut the wages of its workers and a general railway strike resulted, Cleveland ordered four companies of infantry to Chicago to break the strike, and twenty-five people were killed. Theodore Roosevelt, still a few years away from the Presidency, approved such actions: "I know the Populists and the laboring men well, and their faults, . . ." he stated. "I like to see a mob handled by the regulars, or by good State Guards not overscrupulous about bloodshed."

Hannah, shortly after her marriage to Earl Barlow: ca. 1893

Farmers did little better than industrial workers during that depression. In the winters of the nineties they burned their corn for fuel because railroad tariffs and middlemen were taking four fifths of corn profits.

Early in the decade, farmers organized the Populist party. Their platform was radical: public ownership of the railroads and communications systems, abolition of the private banking system, return of corporate lands to the people. In the election year of 1896 the Populists joined the Democrats to nominate William Jennings Bryan for President. He promised to wage a campaign "for the masses against the classes."

That some were rich and most were poor was a result of the free enterprise system, which was, as Andrew Carnegie wrote in 1889, a manifestation of natural law. The solution to the depression, therefore, lay in an expansion of the system—in access to foreign markets. The Spanish-American War, 1898, resulted in the ouster of Spain from Cuba and possession by the United States of Puerto Rico, Guam and, a year later, the Philippines. The twenty-five-year period of depression was over. But not before it had touched Hannah, who, in 1893, married a handsome itinerant laborer whose ability to make a living depended on the general prosperity of the country.

I got married. I thought I was going to be happy. In my own way I guess I was happy for a while. My husband and I lived in Hastings when I got married, and my daddy lived with us, or us with him. Then my daddy and my brother went up north to farm, and me and Earl went out a little way by Earl's people and rented a house. I was with his people more and more. They were quiet people, like my own people were. No carousing and no drunkenness. No, nothing like that. It was just like I was born in the family, they were that good to me.

Earl was their oldest child. He had awful nice, gentlemanly manners and he knew when to use them. And when not to. He must have got in with the wrong gang of people, because he got to be terrible to live with.

Those were the years when there was no work at all. Nothing at all. You was lucky if you could get fifty cents a day. There was no money. Earl managed to get hold of an old horse and wagon and we went around at night catching bullfrogs. I'd spend all night catching frogs and cutting their legs off. They'd be sent to Grand Rapids and sold in shops. And so that way we got something to live on. I wouldn't do it now, but then I was young; I did as I was told.

Earl did have a rich uncle. Uncle Sam was his name. He was an awful wealthy man and sometimes he'd give Earl seventy-five cents a day for work. That was the only work Earl could get. I remember that Uncle Sam wore army clothes, so he must have been in the army sometime or other. You know what he'd do? He'd come to the house with all these dollar bills and have me iron them out. I'd build a fire and heat the iron and chat with him while I'd iron. And then he'd stack up the bills and put them in his pocket and go home. Never even say thank you. I didn't care for that. I'd of cut off my hand before I'd think of taking any of those bills. I'd no more think of taking his money than I'd think of flying!

Well, a year after I was married I had May. She was born at my daddy-in-law's house, and I heard the midwife say, "We'll call it a pound." Now, whether May weighed a pound, or under a pound, I *don't* know. But I guess every woman in town came to the house. They came in bunches and they came single. And I heard them all say, "Oh, she'll never raise *her*. She'll *never* raise her." That child's arm wasn't any bigger than my finger. *I* raised her. I made up my mind I was going to raise her. And she's got four strapping daughters. And grandchildren, she's got. And great-grandchildren and great-great grandchildren. That's that girl. *I* raised her.

I used to live an awful lot at my daddy-in-law's and mother-in-law's in those days when Earl was off working. Or whatever he done. And every night when I'd get May ready for bed my daddy-in-law, he'd come and sit in front of me. And, "Oh, Hannah," he'd say. "You're taking too good a care of that baby. You're giving that baby too good care." My mother-in-law, she'd be sitting there grinning away. She'd let Dad do the talking. But she sanctioned what I was doing. I know, because she sat there with a smile on her face. And I must have been doing all right, because she never gave me any advice. She'd had twelve children of her own, and she had another the same year I had my boy.

I knew some things about babies. I knew that a baby had to be clean and dry. Neither one of my babies ever had a rash on their little butts. Of course I never played with my children. I didn't know you *could* play with children. I never could find anything to say to a child beyond telling them to mind.

My mother-in-law was a fine, fine woman. My, she was grand. Grand cook. And didn't the people like to come there to eat. She had a large family of her own and very seldom did they sit down alone to eat. I don't know how many neighbors come in and put their knees under the table.

When I was visiting there I always washed the dishes. I didn't know how to cook

Hannah:

1893-1898

43

in those days, but washing the dishes meant something because there were so many people eating. And I'd be there visiting so long, three, four weeks at a time because my husband and I never had a place of our own. Always rented. Oh, his people was just like home to me. There was no quarreling. I never even seen their kids quarrel—only the two little ones and my mother-in-law just told them to go out behind the barn and fight it out themselves.

Well, then we left there and went up north. Up near Butterfield Lake in Richmond Township. My husband heard he could get some work up there. He didn't have any particular work he did. He done anything and everything he could do. When he worked, he worked in the woods mostly. That was the work the men went up north for. So we went up there and rented a house just across the road from my daddy and brother.

Well, there wasn't too much work up there. Earl got some farm work and some woods work. But there was a drought in those years, and there wasn't much farm work. Sometimes we had plenty. Sometimes we had nothing. There was a friend of my husband's, and he'd see we had something to eat. And Earl's sister, her husband would see we had something to eat. And that way we got by. I don't know why we had nothing. No work and a lazy man, that was the trouble I guess. Well, I guess there just was no work. Of course the farmers could feed their families, but Earl wasn't a farmer. He couldn't stay still long enough to farm.

Earl did love a good time. He was a great dancer. He'd go to dances even when I'd got May. I'd sit on a bench and lay May down next to me, cover her up. She'd go to sleep and I'd sit there watching the dance. Oh, how he loved to dance! In the middle of the dance everybody would leave the floor and they'd play just for Earl. My, he was a beautiful dancer. Of course I never cared for dancing myself. I didn't know what fun was. I never had what's called a joyous time, no. Never no laughing or fun like that. I had to be sedate.

My boy was born in 1896. I remember I just didn't know what to name him. I liked the name of Cecil so well, but I thought that was a girl's name, so I didn't name him for thirteen months, just called him Sonny. Now I found out later that Cecil *is* a boy's name, but by then Earl wanted to call him Charles.

Now this is something I never told. There was one time I was in the dumps. I had my two babies and they was crying because they was hungry. And I prayed to God, "Oh God, never let me have another child." The life I had with the children's father, I was fed up on it. I didn't want any more children to go half-naked, half-fed. We had more kids that we could feed, more than we could put clothes on. I prayed like that and I never had another child, never got that way again.

My husband said I was a damn fool for having children. *I* didn't think I was. But I didn't want any more. By then Earl had got to be what he was. Did he *drink?* Did he *drink?* I don't know if you'd call it drinking or not. He poured it down. But he never laid a hand on me. When he was himself, he was kind. And he had such grand people!

Well, finally he left me for another woman. It was the eighth of March in ninety-eight when he left me. And she had a husband, so two families broke up. I don't remember what I felt when he went off. Good riddance to bad rubbish, I guess. I don't

45

know. I was so busy with my kids, and being left. Not even any salt in the house.

I feel and I know that I could have gone to his people and stayed with them. But it takes money to travel the whole length of the state, and I didn't have it. And I didn't want to run amuck of Earl. I thought he might be hanging around home. Now, I was *told* this: He'd broke up with this woman and had gone home to his people. He got home and his dad said, "Earl, where's Hannah?" He told. And his dad said, "You get right out and stay out." They never seen him or knew where he was for over ten years. If I hadn't been afraid of running amuck of Earl, I would have gone and stayed with them, just like their own daughter.

From then on I judged all men like Earl. I thought they was all like him. It was a step down, that marriage. I wish I could be elevated back to the class where I belong. The ones that don't belong to your class are the ones that hate you. I used to visit in beautiful homes, that was my class. Then I stepped down, and from then on it was out in the fields, husking corn, picking up potatoes, gathering hay. What haven't I done! Out of my class entirely. I didn't know men. Well, I paid for it. I shed so many tears I couldn't shed any more. I just sobbed.

Hannah: 1898-1908

In March 1898, Hannah moved across the road to her father's farm. She was twenty-two, the "widow Lambertson," as she would be called, with a four-year-old daughter and a two-year-old son.

The house, which was to be her home for the next ten years, had three rooms: a large kitchen and a bedroom on either end of it. The kitchen contained a wood-burning cook stove and a potbellied stove that was kept going day and night in winter. Flour sacks hung in the windows as curtains; a bed, for company, stood in one corner of the room; a rocking chair and wooden chairs around a table completed the furniture. The floors were made of bird's-eye maple, and the wood-board walls were papered.

Outside, at some distance from the house, were the outhouse and the well. The house itself, part log, part frame, faced a sandy road. On the far side of the road a pine woods descended to a lowland and a creek. In back of the house, forty acres were cleared for farming.

It was a time of drought in northwestern Michigan, but the Lambertsons lived where three lakes joined and had water enough to grow food for themselves and their stock. Potatoes were their cash crop, and these they took by horse and wagon to Kalkaska, the nearest large town, about eleven miles away. From there the potatoes were shipped by train to the Chicago markets.

The Lambertsons' was one of the last of the self-sufficient farms. Most farmers had turned to commercial one-crop farming, using the cash from sale of the crop to buy the

47

food and equipment they needed and leaving themselves at the mercy of market fluctuations. It was a farming method that would help create the dust bowl of the next century.

The Lambertsons needed little cash; what the potato crop didn't bring, they earned by doing odd jobs off the farm. It was a life of constant hard work, ten years that Hannah remembers as the happiest of her life.

We was five single folks. My two kids, me, my dad and my brother. But, you know, it was fun. I don't mean having a good sporting time, no. But I guess I should say we was contented. We all had a job. We had our food, we had enough to wear. We wasn't wealthy, but we had enough to feed our stock. We had stock to butcher for our meat. And we had corn in the crib. We had enough and we had a surplus. We had several hogs and we had beef too. And all the chicken we wanted to eat. We drank warm milk night and morning; Dad would come in from the milking and we'd just stand in line and hold our cups out. We used to have chicken just about every other day. And we always had a barrel of sauerkraut, a barrel of pickles and a barrel of sugar and a barrel of salt.

There was a drought in those years, and I guess Dad was probably the only man in Michigan who had a garden. We'd get water out of the lake all day, and when it got dark we'd water the garden. We had a wonderful garden, a luxuriant garden. I remember how we'd be watering and our chickens would follow Dad around while he watered.

Hannah: 1900

Charlie & May: 1900

But those were awful times for some. People had to take their animals out and shoot them because they couldn't grow feed for them. Or they'd give them away to somebody who had a place for them. They had to live somewhere near a lake so there was pasture. I know someone gave Grace Barker a pair of beautiful horses because she lived out near Three Lakes.

Nick got an old boat and I spent my time on the lake. Rowed up and down. I'd take my kids with me, and I'd have so much fun to see how fast I could row. I caught fish and we had those to eat. And we took eels out of the lake. And of course we had other game, like land turtles. I'd row my dad up and down to shoot birds. I was a better shot with a shotgun than a lot of the men. We had red, gray, black and flying squirrels, and I'd shoot them and I never got buck fever.

I was always working and my kids was always playing, crawling around. A lot of my work was at home. I'd bring home washings and ironings. When my kids was in school I'd go out to work. I did washings for the men in the logging camps, and I cooked up in the logging camps, too. It wasn't very far from home and I'd come home nights. There's a kind of lull with farmers, you know, in the winters, and that's the times when I worked out.

I never worried about my kids. They always stayed home. Well, everybody's kids stayed home. I never worried if they'd cross the road, never worried about wild animals. You don't have to be afraid of a bear. They won't touch you if you leave them alone. These two fellows, May and my boy, they was little things. May could walk under a table and her head would never touch it, she was that small. I had a board across the door to keep her in, and she'd stand at the door and call *chi, chi, chi* to the chickens. I'd give her bread to feed them when they'd all come to the door.

And when my kids got older they had their jobs to do. They had to spray the potatoes. And when we went to pick the blueberries we'd leave home at four in the morning and drive to where the berries were. The kids would get down on their bellies and pick as best they could. We'd fill up all the washtubs and come home. We never locked the house up. Nothing was ever touched. Those were good days.

Where I lived, the nearest town that had a doctor was eleven miles away. That's twenty-two miles over sandy roads. So I learned to take care of my kids. Dad bought me a doctor book and also a cookbook. I learned an awful lot out of them. I used to read those quite a bit. Now, one thing my menfolks didn't like was, I didn't know how to cook. One day Dad comes in with a cabbage and he says, "Hannah, you know how to cook a cabbage?" "Well," I said, "you boil it, I guess." That's all I knew was boiling because I seen my grandma do that. But I learned out of the cookbook.

My boy used to have awful sick spells when he was a little fellow. I had a single bed in the front room and I put him there when he was sick. One day Dad come in and looked at him and said, "I think this child's got worms." I got my doctor book and looked it up, and there was a pill for it. So Dad let me take the horse and carriage, and I went to town and got the medicine and give it to him according to what the doctor book said. It *was* worms. He never had any more sick spells. That's how I got along.

Another time I had a chicken that was kind of a nasty color, just about dead. I had nothing to read up on about chickens; I just used dog sense, that's all I had. I

Hannah:
1898–1908

fetched a milk pan, filled it up with water and put a teaspoonful of carbolic acid in it. I don't know where I got the idea, but I fed the chicken with it and, you know, that chicken got well.

I always liked our animals. I talked to them. They learn your words, you know. Our horses, Doc and George, used to come to the door for bread. I'd say, "Want some bread?" And they'd answer, come right up to the door. We had four or five cats; I remember their names to this day: there was Tramp, Tom, Jerry, Teunis and Deal. When I cleaned the chickens there'd be one cat on each of my shoulders watching me clean. And my dog Ti, he used to play with the pigs. And then, at butchering time, how that poor dog did cry, sobbed just like a child.

I was working all the time. I never thought anything about it. Just done it. I never got cross about my work; I never whined about my work. I enjoyed it. I got paid for cooking in the logging camps and doing the men's washing and ironing. That helped pay for what extra we had to buy. But when I went out taking care of the sick, most always the women gave me enough cloth for a dress. That's one way I kept clothed. Oh, yes, I'd learned to sew by then; I had to. And my great-aunt Jane, my grandfather Lambertson's sister—she only had eight years of married life when her man died, been a widow all those years—she used to send us great big packages of goods, old goods, new goods. And I'd make them over. That's how I kept myself covered and my kids covered. You know how they had a long stitch, a short stich to gather up the skirts? Well, that's the kind of skirts she had, and I'd take them down to fit me. But show you how they talk about people! Now, I stayed strictly at home and had no beaux. But I had these goods that Aunt Jane sent me, and there was a piece of farmer's satin—that's satin with a cotton back, not silk. Well, I had a pattern and I made myself a waist and a skirt. It was all black, a black waist and a black skirt. I got reports that people said they didn't see how Mrs. Lambertson could dress so well as she did. All it cost me was the spool of thread Dad bought me. Just a spool of thread.

One time Aunt Jane sent me five dollars and I had bought my boy a pair of overalls. Well, I don't know where he got the idea—he must have found out about starch—and he wouldn't wear his new overalls unless I starched them. So all right, I starched them. He never asked for starched overalls again! And when I wanted him to go barefoot to save out his shoes, oh, I'd get a fight there. He didn't want to go barefooted. But I finally won the day. I like to think on those things. But I don't like to start in and say that I whipped the kids. I don't want the world to know it. Everybody knows that you spank your kids without your telling it. And I just like to think about the good parts. I know it's wrong to whip a child if you're angry, because you hit too hard then. Spank them? Of course I did that. I had to. But there's enough of those things in the world without me telling mine. I don't want the world to know it.

'Course my brother should've whipped those kids. I remember one time he drove eleven miles and back over those sandy roads because he needed wagon grease, to grease his wheels, you know. Well, when he got back he went into the house, and when he came out those kids had used the wagon grease to paint the whole wagon. My, he was mad!

One thing I never did with my kids, I never ran their father down before them. I never have. The kids never knew what I went through with him. I sent my girl down to see her father's people; it was only right they should know her. I sent her down on the train by herself. We took the Hastings paper, so she knew the word Hastings, knew she had to get off and change trains at Grand Rapids. I had put her in the care of the conductor, but she was very reliable, very reliable. And when she got to Hastings her grandma met her. And then I sent her down a second time. I could depend on that girl. She wasn't harebrained.

My boy and my girl wasn't anything alike. The oldest in a family is more dependable than those that come afterwards. Because a parent is liable to say, "Watch the baby, rock the baby." They get to be more dependable than the younger ones are. I didn't make any difference between my boy and my girl. I made all his clothes, I made all hers. They ate the same food, slept the same hours. If you do make a difference between raising them, *you* don't know it. I didn't think any more of one than I did of the other. But when the last one comes, that one has to have the attention. It's a baby; you're accountable for its care. I think every child brings its love with it when it's born. Of course there are people who won't stand for their kids, but they're very few and far between. I think every parent is ready for his child.

One thing I learned about kids: When they're little fellows, never tell them not to do something; if you do, they'll do so. The only thing I told them not to do was not to run from snakes, because I was told not to run from them. I never told my kids not to play with matches, and they never did, never wanted to. I had a friend named Anna Six, Charlie Six's wife. She had two daughters and two sons, and she almost always took them with her when she went to town. But this one day she left them at home. Now, she told me this herself; she said, "I said to the kids, 'You leave those matches alone.' " Well, when she got back they had played with the matches and the little girl's hair had caught fire, and they had to cut it off. So I never told my kids not to do things. Children are ornery; they'll do what you tell them not to. I knew that much about children. This old head of mine, I didn't think it had very much in it, but I knew enough to do the things I was told to do.

And oh, I learned everything. I learned to make sausage. When I got the meat for the sausage all made up, I'd stuff it in those sacks and tie them up. And they'd go up on the roof of the hay barn. And I learned to make headcheese. We had all those things to eat in winter. You keep them in the hay barn, and the hay gives a nice flavor. Oh, I learned to churn. On the farm I had a dasher churn. That's a stone crock, and there's a hole in the cover with a stick goes down inside it—that's your dasher and you churn your cream and get your butter. One time Dad come up from the field and I said, "Dad, suppose you churn awhile." And he did. I don't know how many days later it was, but he made a trip to Kalkaska and he came back with a barrel churn that had a hoop on it. I'd just go like this and get my butter. It was faster, you see. I don't know what made me ask him to churn that time. He might have come up to get his drink of buttermilk, because every time I'd churn he'd have to have his drink of buttermilk. So I asked him to churn it to get it. He had to earn it.

I remember all those things. And when you had buttermilk, well, you put some away for cooking. Pour some water on top of it and that makes a seal all over. You pour that water off and your buttermilk is fine. You do that when you make your sourdough bread too; pour water on top and that'll seal it.

Now, when you husk corn, you have a husking peg. That's a kind of knife, and

55

you set there, cross-legged, and husk your corn. And the husks get left for a couple of weeks before they're gathered. They have to get cured, like hay does. Now, with hay, after it's cut, a man will go every few days and put his hand into it to see how warm it is. When the heat is gone they'll put it up in the hay barn or in a stack. If you don't wait until the heat's gone all out of the hay, it'll catch fire every time. I remember one time after I came out West here, the police were arresting people because a lot of hay burned down. Now, you know a policeman can make anybody believe they've done anything, and they arrested a lot of people for setting fire to hay. But I think that those men didn't know anything about taking care of hay. They put it up too soon. People don't know anymore. They farm out of books; they're not what's called dirt farmers. They don't know. *I* know because I put the hay in windrows and the men put it up in haycocks. I watched them do that. They didn't tell me. I didn't *have* to be told. I knew it'd burn down if the heat wasn't out of it.

Did you ever ride a hay tender? Nothing to it! When your rick is full—it's a great, long rick and it goes around like that and catches the hay—when that gets full, you tip. Then you go along and get another hay load. All those things were fun. They were fun. I loved it. I loved Brown Dick, that was the stallion we had. I loved all of it.

I guess I was as happy in those days as I ever was. I was learning, learning, learning all the time. And I was busy from daylight to dark. They were contented times. I never thought about being happy, I was so contented. I learned to make bread, I learned to make butter, and I learned to make cake and pies. I learned how to sew and make things. I learned to raise chickens. Dad got me an incubator and a brooder and I had just a great time. And when the men was gathering up the corn after it had been husked, I drove the horses on the double wagon around through the cornfields, gathering up the corn. I was busy and I loved it.

Well, I did all those things, and there was always so much in the house I had to do. There was always men there and they were always hungry. My oh my oh my! There was always men around to do the killing of the animals. They'd kill a hog and I'd get the fat cleaned off of the hog intestines to make lard. I was quick at that.

Now, at threshing time, you got to feed all those men. It don't take many men to thresh. There's a man up on the platform that tends to the separating, and a man to tend to the bags. I guess five men would be a surplus. But you have to cook for about thirty or thirty-five. Followers-up, they're called. All the neighbor men and neighbor boys come around at threshing time to get something to eat, to get a good handout, get a good meal, you see. And they want something different from what they get at home. I'd make great big batches of bread and biscuits; they was all great bread-eaters. And in those days we never fried anything; we boiled everything—chicken, porcupine, everything. Dad'd kill some chickens and I'd get that ready in a hurry, and I don't know what other vegetables we had, but I remember we had this great, long table, and about every three feet I'd have a bowl of sliced tomatoes with vinegar and salt and pepper on them, all down the length of that table. Every man that come in just grabbed a fork, never sat down, just started right in on those tomatoes. They acted like they were just starved. I guess everywhere else they went they just had boiled chicken to eat, and there ain't no relish to that.

I didn't mind cooking. I learned out of my cookbook and I never had any trouble.

Nobody ever found fault. When I'd cook I'd take a taste of it every once in a while to see if it was seasoned right. I just got things to taste the way I wanted them to taste. If it didn't taste all right, I'd get it to with a little salt and pepper. If anyone found fault, I didn't know it.

Now, Charlie Eastman and his gang, they boarded at my mother-in-law's cousins', Dick and Ida Powell. Many's the time Charlie would come by. "By God, Hannah," he'd say, "don't you have something to eat?" I'd go to work and get him some breakfast, and he'd go and tell what Ida had given him to eat. He couldn't eat that darn stuff. Oh, she was stingy! She'd brown dough in the oven, no seasoning or salt on it. And she'd have her bread and potatoes all together and no grease on them. Charlie didn't like his food that way.

Charlie was on the railroad gang, you know. One winter, when my boy was a baby, I tended a stationary engine for him all winter. Charlie had had a man to look after it, but he couldn't depend on him. So I did it. Would I know enough to do that now? No! I had to look after all those gadgets, see if they was all working. I can't tell you how I did that now. And another thing I did, I used to keep the scale for logs. The men, they was all smart, they was all businessmen; but they wasn't educated. I didn't know anyone that could read. They had a school there for the younger children, but I was about the only one who knew how to make a figure two. The men always had to have someone do figuring for them. And this fellow, Mark Six, he had a bunch of logs, and he come up to where I was living and he wanted me to keep the scale for him.

I did all those things and I got a little money that way. One winter eggs got high and I sold eggs twenty cents a dozen. And of course Dad sold our potatoes. I always kept track of the market for him, kept track of what potatoes were selling for. I studied up on it and I found out that we always had hard times, bad times, in Republican times. Dad was a Republican and I said to him, "Dad," I says, "how can you be a Republican?" And I told him what I'd learned. He never voted Republican after that.

Of course we didn't need much money on the farm. Once in a great while my great-aunt Jane would send me some, but not very often. I didn't need it. I didn't go anywhere except when I went out nursing. I learned about how to nurse from my aunt Laura. She was a midwife, you know. And her mother, my mother's mother, was a doctor. She could take a case doctors couldn't do anything with, and make them well. So nursing was in my family, you might say. Aunt Laura taught me you have to keep a woman in bed nine days after she has a baby, and when she gets up she can't do any heavy lifting. The doctor would generally come for the birth; there'd be only one woman and the doctor. Men'd just make themselves scarce when babies were being born. They were outside somewhere, hanging around. That's the way it was when I went out nursing.

Now, I want you to know something else about me. I want to tell you how silly I was! Whenever my menfolks was wanting something and didn't want to leave their work, I'd go and do the errand for them. To go to Kalkaska, I'd have to drive the horses, but if they was using the horses I'd walk to Spencer, five miles, and I'd have my apron on to carry my stuff in. Well, one time I was coming back from Spencer. I'd got my stuff in my apron and was coming along by Sam Six's place. Clara Six, his wife, we were good friends and I visited with her too long. Now, there's a section of woods between her road and my road that had a bunch of loggers working there, and it had a cook's shanty. In the spring of the year they cut the hemlock down there and peeled them. So I stayed too long with Clara and by the time I got to the woods it was dark. I just went trotting along. I could keep to the road, because I could tell by the ferns where the road was. I passed the cook's shanty and then it was downhill to get home. While I'd been gone the loggers had felled a log across the road. It showed white—you know how it will with the night-sky light on it—and it was there I heard something trotting along behind me. I'd stop. It'd stop. I'd walk on. It'd walk on. I thought, "It's one of those darn men; he seen me go through and he's trying to scare me." I wasn't very far from home, almost out of the woods, but I turned tail and run up that hill to the cook's shanty. Knocked on the door, and she gave me a cot and I lay down on that and slept till morning. The next morning I got up at daybreak so as to get home and start my breakfast work. I got home and Dad never asked me where I been, never asked any questions. Then, later, the cook come down to get some garden stuff to feed her men, and I seen her talking to Dad. So I went out there and she turned to me and said, "That was a bear after you last night. His footsteps was on that wet log." Well, I'd never looked at the log; it was too high for me to get over it and I had to run in the woods to get around it. Now *there* was the fool thing. If that had been a man after me, when I turned to go up the hill, running, mind you, hard work carrying myself and my apronful of stuff—if that had been a man, he'd a-grabbed me. I never thought about that, oh no! Wasn't that a fool thing I did?

Oh, those were good times. Back there in Michigan you could always tell who was coming down the road. They'd all have their favorite tunes, and you could tell them just as far as you could hear a whistle. They come on down the road, whistling away, hands in their pockets. If you could hear that now, how nice it would be!

I could do almost anything in those days. I only weighed eighty pounds myself, but when I went to town, I'd carry a fifty-pound sack of flour on my shoulder. I didn't think anything of it. The shopkeeper would say, "Hannah, *you* can't carry that." "Why not?" I'd say. "It's paid for, isn't it?" And I'd put the sack on my shoulder, my hand on my hip, and walk right out.

There was a man coming out to the farm to see me in those days, and people told him, "You better be careful of that widow out on the Lambertson place. Anybody that can carry fifty pounds on her shoulder, you better be careful." Well, I just laughed when I heard that.

There was another man used to come out from town. He was a painter, painted houses and things. Nice-looking fellow, fine-looking man. With a moustache. He'd twirl his moustaches and we had more fun about that. Somebody told me, "You better be careful; you always marry the man you make fun of." But we couldn't help it. Didn't we laugh about the way he'd sit there and twirl his moustaches!

When he came out to the farm I didn't visit with him. He visited with Dad and Nick. I just went about my work. It was wintertime and naturally he'd want to feed, but that was all I had to do with him. Well, one time he was looking out the window

61

and he said, "I wonder what those goddamn kids are up to now." My kids was just out there playing. My brother had made them a letter A out of some pieces of board, and they had put a chicken on the crosspiece and was pulling it over the snow. That chicken just sat there. They was always playing with a chicken.

Well, when he said "goddamn kids," if he had any intentions whatsoever, his goose was cooked. I was not speaking to him after that. I guess he didn't know it. He come up and looked at me one time and he said:

It isn't the same old smile you gave me years ago
Something must have happened that is changed you, don't you know.

That was the last time I think I listened to him. I always remember that verse. I didn't have any smile for him after that. Damning my kids! If I'd a married him I'm thinking they'd have had a terrible life. No, no.

There was always somebody coming out to the house to visit. Now, Mr. Humphrey—I nursed his woman, Emmy, when she was sick—he'd come visit and I'd just go about my work. He'd sit there watching me work and he'd say, "Emmy don't do it like that. . . . Why, Emmy don't do it that way." That was about the sum of our conversation. I never did know how Emmy *did* do it. I didn't ask her.

And Jeff Pierson, nobody talked to him. He'd come to the house, take the first chair he come to, look for something to read, pick it up, read it and when he got it read he'd go. Never said anything. Wouldn't know he was in the house. Last time I

seen him, though, he talked a streak. I was scared of him then. *That* wasn't Jeff
Pierson. Talk, talk, talk. "Hannah, I like to talk to you. You got some education."
Talk, talk, talk. I kept looking at one door and then the other, wishing the menfolks'd
come up from the fields. Well, he left after a while, and just four days after that I
heard they put him in an asylum. He was crazy.

My dad wasn't much of a talker. If there was anything to talk about, the farm or
anything like that, he'd talk, yes. I never asked my daddy any questions. Even now,
old as I am, how I wish I'd asked questions. There was so many things I wanted to
know about. I wish I had asked my poor daddy about my mother more. One time he
told me that I looked an awful lot like my mother. I didn't question him. I didn't
contradict. But I had been told that my mother was a beautiful woman. And I was far
from a beautiful woman. I didn't consider I was pretty. I was so afraid I'd hurt daddy if
I asked about my mother. Because he never gave my mother up, you see. Oh, how I
wished sometimes I could hug him around the knees. But I didn't dare to. I was afraid
I'd get him to cry or something. That's what I was afraid of—my daddy's feelings. Not
no wild animals, just my daddy's feelings.

When the telegram come from Uncle Ben, I don't know what my dad did feel
about it. Neighbors brought the telegram as far as they come; and other neighbors
brought it as far as *they* come. It said that Grandma was very low. There was a blizzard
that night and Dad had quite a few miles to walk in the railroad tracks, and then he
had many more miles to walk to Kalkaska to get the train for Hastings. I'd been away
from my grandma so long I worried more about my dad facing that blizzard. When he

come back home and told me she had died, I don't know what I did feel. It wasn't grief. It was just like something had left me. I felt empty. Well, something had gone.

Grandma died a few years before we left the farm and came out West here. That was a few years before I married Mr. Aiken. Matthew Aiken. Matt, I called him. Matt had a sister up here that was married and of course we was acquainted with them. They lived down the road from us. My kids would be out playing in the road and this man would come walking down the road and they played with him. They got so they looked for him. So you could say I met him through my kids.

He was an old bachelor. He was only three years older than I, but he was a bachelor. He was a Christian. What was that sect he belonged to? I can't remember what they called themselves, but they dress oddly. The women, I know, wore a kind of bonnet; and I know he wore a hat. They dressed different. But he was a good man. He didn't drink or anything like that; he didn't carouse. He was my *children's* friend. I used to tease him: "You just married me to get my kids," I'd say. He'd laugh at me, but he didn't say yes and he didn't say no. He thought the world of those kids, and that was good for me.

I want to tell you a funny thing. We was married on the sixteenth of March in 1908. We went to the parsonage and got married, and Dad was waiting for us at the railroad depot. Dad and the man I married got on the train and came West. The bride was left at home. He took my dad on the marriage trip.

I guess they wanted to see the country. So they came out to Washington and they went to some place on the coast. Somebody advised them to come over to Zillah because it was apple-picking time, so they went there and got acquainted with a man called Captain Whippey. He needed help, so they picked apples for him. And several months later they came back home. They brought me some seeds and I planted those seeds. I was here long enough to see the little trees I planted start to come up. I had a plum tree started. I never got to see it bear. I didn't know we had to leave the place, but Dad wanted to go.

See, Dad had improved our place. We had a root house that would hold a carload of potatoes. Dad had built it so it had a driveway between each side and a door on each end. They could drive in and load up their wagon box, and the horse'd go out the other end. And we had a hay barn and a good corncrib. Everything like that. And a pigsty, chicken coop, cow barn, everything. We sold it all. Auctioned off everything. Dad had bought me a new sewing machine and I never got to use it. And an egg brooder. Never got to use that. Everything went. Everything went. All but what we could put in a dry-goods box.

I'll tell you about my daddy, bless him. He was never satisfied long in one place. I guess it was losing my mother. He never got over that. I guess out West he was better satisfied because we'd go from one place to another, one place to another.

Cows on Washington farm

Hannah: 1908-1974

The move to Washington, which Hannah makes her father's personal choice, had also to do with the end of a national way of life. By 1900, prices for farm products were half of what they had been in 1866; more than a third of the country's farmers had become tenants, unable to keep up with the high cost of machinery necessary for increased production. The Lambertson farm, always marginal, relying on a small cash crop and labor off the farm, could not have offered a viable way of life much longer. In 1907, the year before the Lambertsons left Michigan, there was another recession, which waxed and waned until the war boom of 1914.

If Americans had to give up the ideal of economic independence, they were offered another: progress. To move West was progress; to work for wages was progress. This is the way progress looks to Hannah.

I had influence over my dad, but I never used it. If I had to do it all over again, I would oppose leaving the farm. I was happy there. We was all contented. Back home on the farm there was security. We had a home. We raised everything we needed. We didn't have to put our hands in our pockets for everything we put in our mouths, in the children's mouths. We didn't run and buy everything. We raised it. That was an independent life I call it.

The life we had out West, I don't know what you would call it. What wages we could save, we lived up as we went along. We lived everything up, and in the end we had nothing. And the farmers out West—they pay enormous prices for machinery to do the work that men had been doing. That knocks the men with their families out of a job. And the farmers don't stop and think that it costs a lot to keep that machinery up. That's why people are on welfare. That's what done it.

I went from one way of living to another way of living. There wasn't no separation, it seems like. Those were great times on the farm. I loved it. I loved all of it. I guess I left that love behind me when I came out West.

The two-hundred-by-fifty-mile Yakima valley gets only the small amount of rain that slips through the Cascade Mountains; left to itself, nothing but sagebrush would grow in its volcanic soil. But from the Yakima River, which pours out of the Cascades and flows east across the valley to join the Columbia, much of the land has been irrigated. In 1889 the Yakima Canal Company traded two thirds of its stock to the Northern Pacific Railroad for land on which to build an irrigation canal. By 1908, when the Lambertsons arrived, 120,000 acres were under cultivation, and Zillah was a fruit-growing, -packing and -shipping town.

In 1919, Zillah was described this way by one writer:

Among the many stations and villages with their huge warehouses, where the fragrant apples and blushing peaches and equally rosy boys and girls are in constant evidence, those that may be considered the chief towns of the section are Zillah and Granger. . . . Zillah is near the rushing river with its groves of cottonwoods and birches, but is elevated upon a bench

Bottom of the Sunnyside Canal: 1909

which breaks off in an abrupt bank down to the bottomland. From this elevation a superb view embraces within its scope the level expanses of the Reservation across the river, edged with the foothills azure in the distance, while in clear weather the glistening domes of Adams and Takhoma dominate the west and northwest. The laying out of the town was due to one of the foremost builders, Walter N. Granger, originator of the Sunnyside Canal. . . . The name was given the town for Zillah Oakes, daughter of the president of the Northern Pacific Railroad Company.

Beyond any other town of the valley, Zillah might be said to have the big railroad men and promoters of the period as its sponsors.

Hannah's response to Zillah was not so glowing. She found the snow-covered domes of the mountains hidden behind a haze of dust and heat; swarms of flies and malaria-bearing mosquitos; wages of ten cents an hour for packing the apples and for catering dinner parties for Walter Granger.

Well, we came West. We got on the train in Kalkaska and we had to go to Chicago and transfer to the train to come out here. I think we made the trip on fifty dollars apiece. It was some sort of special rate, I know that. They tried their best to get us to stop off in Montana, but Matt, no, he wanted to come to Washington, so we came.

We got off the train at Toppenish on the first day of November in 1908. And we started to walk from Toppenish to Zillah. That's about five miles. I remember I had a fur jacket on and I wasn't used to such warm weather. And walking! You know this soil out here is what's called volcanic ash. And it's just as level as that tabletop, just as level as can be. Well, I'd take a step and my foot'd go way down; there'd be a hole there and I'd never know it. And I'd take another step and it'd be a bump. A bump's a hole upside down, you know. Oh, I had a great time learning to walk! So we were walking, and a man came along with a horse and carriage and he took me and May up and took us to Zillah. He was a preacher there, and his wife was preaching at Toppenish. We rode with them to Zillah and went to the hotel there and waited for the menfolks to come along on foot.

I'll tell you something about that hotel. Talk about flies! Nary a screen. An open tank of water in the kitchen, no cover to it. Matt called it fly soup and he got awful sick from it. The people who owned the hotel was called Furman—Mrs. Furman and Grandma Furman and their daughter Mildred. Mildred done the cooking. She dipped right out of that water covered with flies. And I seen her peeling apples for sauce. She'd come to a rotten spot in the apple and it went right in her sauce. I can laugh about it now, but it wasn't a laughing matter then.

When I first came to Zillah there wasn't any sidewalks. There was a couple of grocery stores and a blacksmith shop and the hotel. They had a good school though, and a Christian Church and a waterworks. And on Sundays they'd ride bucking horses in the corral. They used to have malaria fever out here a lot. Took a lot of people off. Almost took my boy off. When I was working out packing apples, he got the malaria fever. The man I worked for let me have a tent put up in the orchard so my boy would be close by and I could tend to him. More than once I thought he was dead.

Hannah:

1908-1974

71

There were already quite a few orchards here in those days. The Sunnyside Canal wasn't very old, but you put water on this volcanic ash and you can grow just about anything there is. Up above the canal, where they couldn't get water, it was all sagebrush. People would burn it for fuel; it burns real hot, you know, and everything smells of it. Then, a few years later, they put in the Roza Canal, way above the Sunnyside, and that irrigated the land in between.

After we'd been out here a week or two, Dad and Nick got a place down by the canal, and me and Matt rented one down in the village. It was more a shanty than a house. That was Zillah. Just a board shanty, you might say, two rooms on the bank of the Yakima River. The river was seventy-five feet straight down, but that didn't bother me any. While we was living in that house they put a train right out in front. I tell you I got a lot of fun out of that train. It was only one coach, and the windows were portholes, like they are in a boat. When that train got, oh, quite a ways off, they'd make it say hello. It was hello to me. I was the only one on the riverbank. *Hello,* that train whistle would say.

Right across the street from me was Doc McCracken's office. Sometimes the Indians would come by there. I think he sold them whiskey. There were lots of saloons in Toppenish, but of course they weren't allowed to sell to the Indians. There used to be hundreds of Indians sitting on the sidewalks in Toppenish. Just sitting, all humped up in their blankets. I guess they didn't have anything else to do. There'd be a bunch of elderly women sit on the streets. Not the young ones. But there's some beautiful young ones. My, they were beautiful! They had the Yakima Indian Reservation out by

Toppenish, but of course a lot of the land had been leased to white people, and they cut about four or five crops of hay a year on it.

I didn't have May with me. She was over with her aunt in Tacoma, I think. I did have my boy. He went to school in Zillah. There were a lot of Greeks out here building the Northern Pacific and he hobnobbed with them quite a bit.

My first work out here was with Captain Whippey. That was my first work, learning to pack apples. I learned to sort them and pack them. You know the people I packed apples for? The Tiffanys. They had been my grandaddy's friends, the people Grandad always hobnobbed with—Tiffanys, Wanamakers, I can't think of all their names—the ones that used to come to the farm to visit Grandad. And this here man, Cap Whippey, who taught me to pack apples, he used to be the Tiffanys' yacht captain. And his wife used to be the tutor for their children. So here I was packing apples for my grandad's friends at ten cents an hour!

Well, I packed all fall. In those days they didn't have winter shifts like they do now, so when packing was over with, I went working out by the hour. There was a lot of women worked at hop picking, but I never went into the hop fields. Of course there's more money in that than there is in packing apples.

Dad and Matt worked on the canal mostly. It wasn't very old then and it had to have a lot of work done on it. Matt worked most of the time on the repair shift. And Dad did riprapping—that's keeping the banks all right. You want to know the silliest thing? They had one job down in Sunnyside—that's the other end of the canal—and Matt would be sent down to Sunnyside, and the man in Sunnyside would be sent up to

73

Zillah. Wasn't that the silliest thing that ever was? But that's the way that boss was. Matt wasn't home very much. He was away working on different places on the canal, and I was working out for ten cents an hour.

What did I do? What didn't I do! I done everything but fly to the moon. I did midwivery when the cases come up. I got paid more for that, of course. Midwivery was more money. But you had to go out and buy everything. Down on the farm we had everything to eat. Out here you had to go down in your pockets and buy everything. Out here there was no silver money, only nickels, no pennies. You got paid in gold for everything. And when the government changed it to paper money, was the people disgruntled! Old paper trash!

I washed clothes over the washboard. I ironed. I mopped. I took out rugs and shook them. I turned mattresses. I cooked. Of course back home in Michigan I done all those things on the farm. But since I been West it's been for every Tom, Dick and Harry.

I catered big meals for Mr. Granger. He was the head of the Sunnyside Canal, you know, the one who got it put through. They always had big parties, called themselves the Zillah Four Hundred. They was the aristocrats of the town, see? When I catered for them I heard them say, "Why, you'd think she was one of *us*." Chances are I had better training than any of them did. I was always catered *to*. I never had to cater till I came West.

But I liked to work; I learned something all the time. When I worked in the hotel I used to have to run the hotel myself a lot of the time. I had to do the marketing and I had to do the cooking, and I had to wait on tables and wash dishes. I did the

Nicholas, Hannah, & William: 1910

Matt Aiken 1928

Matt on hay wagon: 1919

Matt & William (Dad) in strawberry patch: 1922

whole thing. And I got on all right. When you run a hotel, you have to know what every piece of food costs; whether it's a piece of potato or a chop, you have to know. I had that all down. But I didn't make any more when I catered big parties than when I was over the washboard. Ten cents an hour. And then there was a time, later on, when I did janitor work at the Masonic Hall and the Christian Church. Matt helped me some with that when he wasn't working.

Matt was a better husband than my first husband in all ways. He didn't drink and carouse around. And another thing, he was used to getting meals. He had lived with his parents for many years. His mother was aged and he looked after her. And he took care of his father for seven years. Now, that's what he *told* me. I don't *know.* So in the mornings he'd sneak out of bed and I'd hear him, he'd be busy in the kitchen. *"I'll* get breakfast," I'd say. "Can't *I* get it?" But my, he could make grand biscuits. He was a southerner, you know; he could beat me any day.

The only thing about him, if he was out of a job he was uneasy. He wasn't a trained man, just a day laborer, you see. Just like all the rest. But he was never cross. He was French and Irish. You know what that combination makes, don't you? A hot temper. But he never abused me with his temper at all. One day he was in a temper and I went and stood in front of him. I don't know what I said; I just said some fool thing and he said, "My God, Hannah, I wish you'd do that every time." So every time I seen he was angry I'd make some fool remark to him. That's all there was to it. That was all our quarrels amounted to.

I always honored my menfolks. I know there's some women that's the devil to live with. The women I've seen out here are not like they were when I knew them back home. Tyrants, an awful lot of them. They're the ones that know everything. The *man* don't know anything. How's a man like that? I've seen an awful lot of unhappy men. You can tell by their faces, you know. Women don't keep their marriage vows. Women should keep their place. A woman's place is in the home, trying to make a pleasant place for the man she married. She takes the vow that she'll love, honor and cherish him, and then she don't. She dishonors him. "I'm boss," I heard one woman say that. *"I'm* boss." That's no home life. If she gives a sign, the man talks; if she don't, he keeps quiet. He's got no freedom, no nothing. That's not the way my folks were. There was none of that snarling. No woman can run a man's business. If she thinks she can, she's a nitwit. A woman's got no business to lord it over a man. She's going against God's plan. He made woman for the man; he didn't make man for the woman. That's what the Bible says.

Now, I worked out because I didn't have anything to keep me busy at home. Matt was always away working. And I didn't stick my nose into his business. Never asked any questions, where he went or anything like that. I never knew where Earl Barlow was, but I always knew where Matt Aiken was, because he always told me. And I worked out because I was alone all the time and it's better to have work than idle hands. The devil finds plenty for idle hands to do.

Well, I had a lot to do. And so much happened. Everything happened. After a couple of years out West, we went back to Michigan, and the menfolks cut logs back there. But then Dad wanted to come back here. "I'm going to be buried out West," he

Dad, Charlie & friend, Matt & Hannah: Algona, 1921

Hannah: 1922

Hannah: 1925

said. He wasn't old yet, only fifty-three, but we came back out to Zillah. And then a few years later, we bought a farm out by the town of Roy, but we couldn't make a living on that. So then we went to Algona, and Matt worked out there in the woods. And Dad was always with us. I don't know where the years went. And oh, there were some hard times, some awful times.

I nursed Matt for two years before he died. He had what's called apoplexy. One time, when we lived in Zillah, I was on the backside of the bed and he was trying to get up. He got his feet up, but he couldn't get the rest of his body up. He couldn't move, couldn't get up. Well, that passed, and he was all right. So years later, when we was living in Algona, he was trying to get up, and I thought he was doing the same thing he did so long ago in Zillah. "Matt," I says, "what's the matter?" *Mmmmmmm,* that's all the poor fellow could say. Then I got scared. I got out of bed. He'd been trying to light the fire and he fell on the stove. *Mmmmmmm,* that's the sound he made. The doctor said that his left side was dead.

Matt was a big man, weighed a hundred ninety-eight pounds. And that man would fall down and I'd help him get up. *How'd* I do it? It wasn't *my* strength. What a time I had! And just before he died—he knew, you know—he said, "The Lord's coming after me," and oh, he looked so happy. And it wasn't very long before the Lord did take him. He just went to sleep like a baby. That was December in 1928. Matt died. Nice Christmas present, wasn't it? He'd been an invalid for two years and he got so he could talk pretty good. I didn't miss taking care of him, but I missed him being around.

83

Episcopal Church in Zillah: 1925

Hannah & Matt in
Algona, shortly before
Matt died

There are some things I remember when they happened, but other things I can't remember when. Now, there was a time out West here when there was no work. You couldn't buy anything. The Red Cross helped us out. There was a woman by the name of Mrs. Sleet. "Oh, you'll get used to it," she said. But I never did. No, I never did. Your food was handed out to you. The cloth to make your clothes with was handed out to you. You'd cry your eyes out, you couldn't buy anything. Those were hard times, hard times.

I never did very much voting, but my belief is Democrat. Always had a hard time in Republican times. No money, no work, no nothing. People's got to have work. The laboring class had got to have a job. He's got to feed his family. The children have got to eat. That's what makes some people steal. I don't know, but I should think it would. I don't approve of it, but if I had a bunch of young ones that was hungry, I think I'd have to steal.

There was one time, the Depression time it was, I was living right across from the railroad tracks, down to Auburn. And the men would come and want something to eat. And I'd fix them a meal. You know what they'd do? They'd leave their moniker—a sign to the next men who come, to show who will feed them so they don't go to the wrong house and get turned away. I don't know how many of those fellows I fed. The church I belonged to then, we'd make up big baskets of stuff, sandwiches and things, and take it over to an open field where the men was camping. And we'd sing. I remember there was two preachers among them. My folks had plenty then, but there were those who were hungry. I'd always give them a plate. They had the same as I had—potatoes, lard, whatever I had. It was awful times.

Hannah:
1908-1974

85

I don't know what happened to all my friends I had in those years. I lost track of them all. I moved too much. In Zillah I had a lot of Indian friends. They'd camp in my yard and I used to take some food to them. They'd give me beads; they'd want to give me something. I used to have a good time talking to them and I could say, now and then, a word in their language. I thought an awfully lot of them. And I used to have a few Negro friends as well. I had a Negro neighbor, a perfect lady. My son and her husband worked together, and she used to go into Toppenish quite often. Well, one day I said, "Mrs. Allen, when you're going into Toppenish someday, can I go with you?" "Indeed you can't!" she says. "Well," I said, "Mrs. So-and-So goes with you, why can't I?" "Mrs. Aiken," she says, "there's a lot of white people got more nigger blood than I got." She didn't consider I had any nigger blood in me, see; so I couldn't ride with her. I never asked her again.

You know about Negro babies, don't you? They're born white, you know. The blacker that baby turns out to be, that's how white it is when it's born. I went down the hill to see Mrs. Allen's baby when she had it. It was the prettiest little thing: little pink hands, little pink feet. Didn't look like a Negro at all. And that child turned out as black as black could be.

I never did have any children with Mr. Aiken. I was still young enough, but I didn't because of how I told you I prayed to God that time when my kids was babies. And one time, during the hard times, a married woman whose husband had no work told me this: At nighttime, when you're ready for bed, you have your douche ready with warm water and one tablespoon of vinegar. Use that douche before you get into

Dad & Hannah: Algona, ca. 1928

Nicholas

Charlie feeding bear on
Mt. Rainier, 193

bed. And if you keep that up every night you'll not have any babies. Mr. Aiken thought about children, thought about adopting one. But we never did; and then, when I was up in my forties, I guess it was, we got May's four girls to take care of.

May and her husband separated, you know. Well, he was no good. I told her so in the first place. She met him at her aunt's, and when she got home from there she had his picture in the back cover of her watch. She showed it to me, and "May," I says, "I don't think you want to marry *that* fellow." "Oh," she says, "why not?" "Well," I says, "he's got a terrible temper." "You're always ready to talk about somebody!" She snapped that back, so I never said anything more.

They got married and I never asked her how she got along. I never poke my nose into my folks' business. I don't know anything about their affairs and I never asked any questions. But after she was married to him for a while, she said, "Ma, what you said about Ernest's right." Oh, he had a diabolical temper. Well, he was a mamma's pet; you know how a mamma's pet generally turns out. He was lazy. Oh, he couldn't pick fruit, because the ladder hurt his feet and made his back hurt. He was a baby. He never growed up.

He left her for another woman, just like Earl Barlow left me. I never thought about that before, but it was the same thing. And May had four girls, blondes all of them. I took care of them after her husband left her because she had to work out in the laundry.

I remember when May was a little kid, not in school yet, she was playing on the floor and she said, "When I get big and I have a little girl, I'm going to call her

Grace." I don't know where she got that name, but she did call her first girl Grace. Then there was Annabel, Irene and Margaret. I took care of them till Matt took bad with his stroke—I don't know how long that was, about four or five years, I guess. The two oldest girls, even Irene, they earned their board. They had little jobs before school, like working for a minister's family. They've all done pretty well. Four strapping girls. Grace is the slimmest of the bunch. Irene is the smallest. Annabel and Margaret, they're mammoth women. I think they take after my mother-in-law; she was a large woman.

Annabel, she worked in a laundry quite a while. And then she got another job somewhere. She buried one husband, was a widow awhile, and married another one. Grace, she's always worked in the laundry. She can't work now. She's living on social security; she lived on the state a long while, too. And the third girl, Irene, she's got her first husband, the only one she married. She's the only girl that has. I'm proud of her. She done better than I did. Done better than her mother. But I don't know much about the girls since they left me.

After Matt died, I had my dad. Dad and Nick had always stayed together until Nick got married in his old age. Well, I *say* old age. He must have been about forty, and he had ten children. I was never in no hurry to get married. I didn't marry Matt until my boy was twelve years old, and after Matt died I wasn't in a hurry to get married again. Dad and I did a lot of traveling at about that time. We made a trip with another family to Arkansas. We went to revival meetings, a lot of them. I don't remember where we went or how many we went to. But I remember thinking when we

Hannah with "Jesus Saves" guitar: 1936

Tom Nesbitt & Hannah:
Cohalis Beach, 1938

got back here to Washington, "Oh, how *good* these foothills do look." These are not mountains around here, you know. They're foothills. I have lived, you might say, in a pocket of the Cascades. These mountains are just wonderful.

I got married to Tom Nesbitt ten years after Matt died. It was in thirty-seven, I think it was. I married him for companionship, to have somebody to talk to. I had more companionship from the cat than I got from him. He never talked. He sat there just like he was lost, lost in his own dreams, I guess, I don't know. Tom Nesbitt lived in a different world. He set there and you could talk to him and he'd never hear you. Daydreams, pipe dreams. Never had any conversations with him. Never got through his dreams. Old man, smoking his pipe and dreaming dreams of the past. I guess I've had my pipe dreams too.

I don't know anything about what Tom Nesbitt was. I know he was called a doctor by some people. And I know he was called Colonel by some people. What he was, I don't know. Once when we were traveling back east with my boy Charlie, he met a friend. "Hello, Colonel," the man said. "How are you? Long time no see." I don't know if it was a nickname he had. I didn't ask him. He just went around with men's britches on, that's all I know. He was retired when we got married; we didn't marry till we were up in our sixties.

He was a good musician, my last man was. We had a mandolin and a piano. If you didn't ask him, he was a good singer. If you asked him he wouldn't sing nothing. I was always crazy for music. I used to tease my grandma for a piano, but she said her daughter didn't have one, so I couldn't.

I know Tom had traveled a lot. He'd been in every state but one. And he read a lot too. When neighbors come in he'd talk. He'd tell people where he'd been. And I'd say, "Tom, why don't you talk to *me* like that?" I'd go stand in front of him and I'd stick my hands on my hips, like this. I had a picture of myself in my mind; I know how I looked. "Why *don't* you talk to me?" And I didn't say it very nice either. He'd grin, settle back. I never got anything out of him.

I could tell a whole lot of stories, but I don't believe in that. The only thing my kids knows about Mr. Nesbitt is that it was no picnic to live with him. He was no angel to live with. I don't say *why.* It was my life. I married him. I made a fool of myself. He *was* a gentlemanly man, very gentlemanly. Very attractive-looking man. But what's the use of that? Now, I made a mistake in my third marriage. I thought I was getting more than I got. Get someone to care for me, that's what I wanted more than anything else. Because nothing's ever satisfied this awful hurting and longing I had. It was an ache. For my mother. That's why I couldn't bear to be around my schoolmates with their mothers.

I never told about that longing. I didn't know what it was until this winter. I asked God, "God," I prayed, "is that longing for my mother?" I named it, and He took it away. I haven't had it since. That awful hurting, that longing. That's what led me to marriage. But my husbands never touched that longing.

I guess I was more at ease with Dad than with anyone else. But, you know, I don't think I ever hugged my daddy. Just when he died. He was in Charlie's garden, hoeing, and I made him quit. He set on the front porch there, visiting awhile, and a day later he died. His heart gave out. He died in my arms. That was the hardest thing to happen. I just couldn't stand it. He was eighty-six when he died.

Tom Nesbitt & Hannah: Yakima, 1946

Hannah & Tom at Pendleton Round-up, 1945

After my daddy died, that was during the Second War, I think, me and Tom and Charlie were traveling around a lot then. Charlie had a fretsaw and he cut out names from wood—names and Indian heads and things like that. He put pins on the back of them and sold them. He sold in Yakima, and then we'd all go together down to the rodeo in Pendleton, Oregon, and sell there. We made a trip to Ohio, going around selling those things Charlie made. And different places in Michigan. Tom and I did that some years. He died in 1960. I been alone now fourteen years.

Tom had a bad heart, you know. And I think, by the odor, he had a cancer. We were living in Yakima then, and we had an inside toilet, a portable one. I did my best to keep that odor down. Talk about odor! It'd knock you known. I took care of that man, lifting him, turning him, doing for him. And it was just too much for me. I got so bad I could hardly put one foot in front of the other. The doctor come up and says, "I'm gonna take Tom to the hospital and X-ray him." The next thing I knew he was in a nursing home. He was there just one week and he died.

I've been alone ever since. When I was a widow the first time, I had my daddy and my brother; then, when Mr. Aiken died, I still had my daddy. Now I've got no one. I'm a pauper. Don't that make Charlie mad when I say that! "You're not a pauper," he says. "Anything you get over the counter you pay your taxes on it." I say that don't make any difference. I'm not living on my own. And I have to have those snoopers from welfare. They come in your house; they go look in your cupboards and everywhere else to see what you have. They have no right to that at all. One woman, she cut my pension six dollars. She says, "You can eat spinach. Spinach is good

Hannah:

1908-1974

97

eating." Well, I don't *like* spinach. One time I thought I got a raise in pension. I got a check for a hundred fifty-five dollars and four cents. But what it was, I had to buy my own food stamps. Before, the state was buying my stamps. I never asked the state for anything. I have never found fault if they cut me, and I've never said anything when they raised me. But you know what hurts? Folks are ashamed of you. They look down on you. They'll take you to the back alley to go into a store. They look down on me because I'm on welfare. It's a mighty good thing. It's better than the poorhouse when I was young. I'd work if I could, but I've got to the age where no one will hire me.

You know, my people, on my mother's side, are royalty-descended. And my kids, on my first husband's side, are royalty-descended too. Talk about royalty! It's a pipe dream. Old clothes given to me. Living on the state. Isn't it a joke? *I* call it a joke.

It's Job I'm descended from. I've had a few of Job's troubles. I appreciate how patient he was with all his sufferings. I have to be like Job and keep my mouth shut. I'm not angry, but I'm heartsick.

I had a bad fall last spring, you know. My legs just went out from under me and I lay there crying for help. That cat just sat at my head and yowled. Well, the neighbors found me and then May come out to take care of me. Next day May broke her wrist, and she said she couldn't take care of me and my dog. She had that dog put to sleep. You know what my dog's name was? Utell. That was like what my grandmother named her dog. She named him Guess, and every time somebody'd come to the house and ask what the dog's name was, she'd say Guess. Oh, they guessed all kinds of names. One time the caseworker came to my house. "What's your dog's name?" she said. "Utell," I says. "*I* can't tell," she says.

Hannah: ca. 1965

Earl Barlow in Michigan: 1955

Well, I betrayed Utell. I'd taken care of her so tenderly for so long, and she just trotted off with May like she was going somewhere. I betrayed her trust. May's hard as nails.

I don't want to live on my children for anything. I've got lots of relatives that are millionaires. But I'm nothing to them and they're nothing to me. I don't go around whining and telling them who I am. Maybe they'd believe me and maybe they wouldn't. Lots of heartbreak in this life. It's an awful test. I call myself Job sometimes and I'm not giving my God up. When he sees fit to lift this curse, I'll be better off. But when that will be, I don't know. Last time I cried, I couldn't shed a tear. I've cried enough tears to swim in, but they won't come anymore.

I know I was well bred. Well educated. All the niceties of life. That's my grandmother's doing. She raised me that way. But that don't mean anything. That don't spread your bread. I'm old and only in the way right now. I *am* in the way. And I know I am by the things that are said to me. But what can I do about it? Oh, I have self-pity so much it doesn't do any good to mention it.

I've always been sorry I didn't have some kind of trade. So I could have been something. Instead of being over the washboard, scrubbing the floors. All those I worked for been dead many, many years. One woman, she was a beautiful woman, she's dead many years. I guess her children are dead now too. I'm still here. Why? I don't know *why!* Does God have something for me to do? We're not here for nothing, you know.

I want to tell you something. My first husband had gone to the hospital—it was some years ago, I don't remember when. But I didn't know this; I didn't know anything about him since he left me. But starting in June, I felt something stumbling against my bed. Ruby tried to tell me it was just the trucks going by, but something made me pray for Earl. And that November I just had to drop everything and pray and bawl and pray and bawl. I didn't even know he was sick. I didn't know what it was all about till we got the obituary that said he died in November. He came back to me after leaving the way he did.

I'm talking too much. Nobody to talk to. Nobody comes. I've told you everything I know about my life. It's been work, work, work and move, move, move. There's nothing remarkable ever happened to me. I was just like any other kid, wandering around by myself, going to school and coming home. And when I married I just tagged around wherever my husband went.

My daddy's buried in Yakima. My mother's buried in Michigan. My brother's buried in the foothills west of Auburn. I don't know where I'll be buried yet. I hope it'll be far away from this place. I want out of here so bad it makes me sick. Cry, cry, cry. You know, I wished I lived somewhere near Tacoma, or someplace. I'd get a housekeeper. I don't need one to do my work, just for companionship. And I'd have a car and when she'd be going out to do my trading, I'd say, "Me wanna go too." Sounds just like a baby, don't it?

Life is funny, very funny. And yet it's serious, very serious. I can't understand why the world should go the way it does.

May

```
                              William Lambertson ──────┬────── Eleanor Ogden
                                                        │
                                   ┌────────────────────┴────────────┐
                                   │                                  │
        Earl Barlow ───────┬─────── Hannah                      Nicholas
                           │
                ┌──────────┴──────────┐
                │                     │
Ernest Hochman ──┬── May           Charles
                 │
      ┌──────────┼──────────┬──────────┐
      │          │          │          │
    Grace     Annabel     Irene     Margaret
```

May

Hannah's daughter—the baby who weighed a pound at birth, the child who wasn't "harebrained," the girl who married a bad-tempered man and had four daughters—is eighty years old. This confrontation with the passage of time is breathtaking.

May is so distant a presence in Hannah's account, misplaced for long periods of time, that her reality comes as a surprise. She is, in fact, a definite presence: a stout, white-haired, robust woman who could pick up her mother and carry her as easily as she would a baby. But if the eighteen years that separate them have, physically, reversed their roles, May, for all her eighty years, is a daughter still.

Seeing Hannah through May's eyes, the focus blurs and changes; mothers are different women to their children than they are to themselves. Hannah understood her obligations to her children as simple, if not always easy: to keep them fed and clothed, and as obedient as possible until they were grown. She did not know, as she said, that you could play with children or talk to them. That she loved them, she took for granted; if a mother did not love her children she would not take good care of them. But May, like Hannah, laments the lack of her mother's love. It is a complaint echoed by each Lambertson daughter. Mothers and daughters went through life with the most important things between them unspoken.

May lives alone, on an income from social security, in a pleasant housing development about twenty-five minutes by bus from downtown Tacoma, and about 175 miles from Hannah. The one-story, boxlike houses, with slanting roofs, are surrounded by neat lawns and flower beds. The development, originally built for defense workers during World War II, is operated by the Tacoma Housing Authority; rents are adjusted according to income, and services are provided for older residents. May occupies one-half of a two-family house, a bright, clean apartment with comfortable upholstered furniture. Her one luxury is a large console color television set. When I came to see her in the mornings I usually found her sitting in an armchair with her miniature poodle on her lap, watching a program. On the second morning I came, we watched together while Richard Nixon made his maundering farewell to his staff. "I hate to admit it," May said, "but I voted for him last time." Her explanation is interesting for what it says about the value of the familiar and the acceptance of limits to the possible: "We'd had Nixon long enough to know what he would do. We knew he was a crook. But McGovern seemed to be so radical. He said he was going to go over and talk to the Vietnamese people and get our boys home right away. Well, we all knew he couldn't do that."

May does not have her mother's sense of tragedy or poetry of language. Her style is different. There is something of New England in the wry, terse quality of her speech; it is more than just a mannerism, it is an attitude that seldom falters, a cheerful matter-of-factness about life.

In May's account of her life—as in Hannah's—the years after youth tend to merge into one another, with little sense of a gradual passage into middle and old age. The young girl, with her unarticulated hopes for the future, becomes a wife, and quickly a mother, then a worker, absorbed in the repetition of daily tasks. Time, which was marked in the early years by the newness of life, of marriage, by the birth of children, settles into routine, the years distinguished only by the largest events.

Most of May's working life was spent in a commercial laundry. She liked her job, liked the contact with other people it brought her, and liked, most of all, having money of her own. The quality she values most in herself, and in others is independence—financial and emotional, and the first leads to the second. "When I had a job, nothing worried me," she says about the time she separated from her first husband. When pressed, she admits to sadness, but she treats it with wonder and resentment, like an intruder unnecessarily complicating simple facts. I asked whether she misses her second husband, who died, and she says, "Oh yes. I miss my car too." She laughs about giving both losses equal weight, while her fingers drum an agitated rhythm on her coffee cup. But she will not give into the nonsense of emotion. It gets you nowhere. Her life has been what it has been; she has friends and family with whom to play Bingo and pinochle, and she accepts what she can deal with.

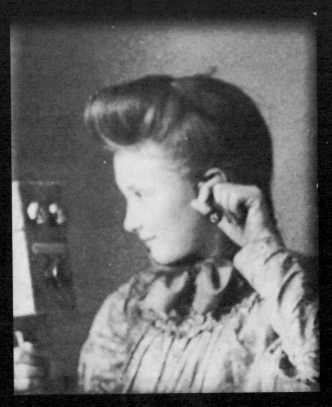

*May on the telephone:
Michigan, 1905*

May: 1894–1908

First that I can remember about anything was when I was about four years old. We lived in a log cabin just off from a crick, up in the northern part of Michigan. It was nice in those days, mostly woods. There used to be panthers down by the crick. I remember one time my mother thought one of them was a woman crying.

Our house didn't have no clearing around it, because my father never done any farming. He worked in the woods, I guess. We used to have kerosene lamps and I think we brought our water up from the crick. We had two stoves; one was for heating the place, and the other was for cooking. I wished I had one of them now. It seems like things tasted different then when my mother cooked all of our meat and vegetables and baked our bread on that stove. I imagine my father must have hunted our meat because I know we didn't raise any. I think we had a dog and I know we had a cat, because she had a litter of kittens and I said I wanted the black one. That cat packed all her kittens away, brought back the black one for me, and she went away and never came back again. It was a funny thing.

My father left when I was about four. The day he left he made me catch the only chicken we had, so he could help eat it before he left. I didn't know he was leaving till he was gone. That's all I remember about it.

We moved in with Grandad right away after that. My grandad's house was right across the road from us. The front room and the room where we slept was boards, not logs, and there was a kitchen that had been built on, and a bedroom made of logs.

Grandad and my uncle Nick slept in the bedroom, and my mother and us kids slept in the other end of the house, off the front room. I remember my mother had a picture of her mother hanging on the wall in there.

My mother was skinny as a rail. Little and skinny. She's always telling us her hair was reddish, but I remember it as dark brown. She always wore it put up. She was a hard worker, always was. She scrubbed those floors good, kept them just as white as white could be; you could just see the little white eyes in the wood. And I remember she made some scatter rugs for the floor.

It was cold in the winters. Sometimes it got down to fifty below. I remember my grandad would be up first in the morning to make up the fires, and my mother and us kids would get up after the fires was going good. The outhouse was quite a ways from the house and, boy, that was a cold trip! And the well was quite a long ways too. My uncle made a yoke to put over his shoulders, and he hanged buckets from it to pack the water up to the house. There wasn't much to do in the wintertime. We played at home mostly and other kids would come and play at our place. My mother wouldn't let us go to other people's houses; she kept us at home where we belonged so that she would know what was going on.

We were awful as kids. I remember one time I put on a pair of my mother's shoes, put a stick in my mouth and went outside and fell down and ran the stick down my throat. Another time the wagon wheels was all frozen. They had iron bands around the wheels, and I put my tongue out on one of those bands and it stuck fast. Usually we played around outside with our hand sleds, and we played in the house, teared the house down. Us kids used to take chairs and turn them upside down and make believe they were our train. And we'd play my uncle's phonograph; it was one of those that had cylinders for records—band music, stuff like that.

My mother made me one of those big rag dolls that come on a pattern and you cut them out and stuff them. But mostly we'd make our own toys. In the summertime we'd make a fence around a little piece of ground and take different color rocks and pretend they were chickens inside the fence. Then, we always had a chicken that was our pet, and we would take it around in our sled or wagon. We'd just choose one chicken to play with, and it would come and sit with us at night until I would take it out to the coop. We never made pets of the little pigs, because you knew what was going to happen to them. Then, back in one of the fields, there was a big rock, tall as a house. Us kids used to go back and ride it, call it our horse. It wasn't rocky country; nobody knew how it got there. My uncle once dug down, trying to find the bottom of it. He never did.

I started going to school when I was about six. Us kids had to walk two miles to school. We never got lost, because back there you knew where you was at because the land was all laid off in sections; everything was square, no curves. There were townships and you knew just where you were. In wintertime the snow was so deep you couldn't even see the fences, and there would be a crust on top of the snow, so you could walk right over it on top. If you got a thaw you would have to go by the road.

That school was just one room, and all the children had one teacher. There were about ten or twelve children. My mother had taught us our ABCs and all that sort of stuff before we even went to school. In those days the teacher didn't want to bother with stuff like that. We had to stay at our desks and behave ourselves. No talking. We had to study and answer when we were called on. No foolishness. My brother had *more* dunce caps on his head! And he was always having to sit in the corner.

I behaved myself. I never got the ruler like he did. In those days when kids got punished in school they generally got punished at home. When my mother found out my brother had been punished, she punished him. If he couldn't behave himself in school it was just too bad. One time he put a bunch of little snakes in a pencil box and turned them loose in school. He was always up to something.

My brother was a real daredevil. He'd do everything. The day he cut off his thumb my mother had gone to town. It was in April, I remember, and there was still a lot of snow on the ground. She had gone in the parson cutter—that's the same as the buggy, only with runners on it. That day my brother was so mean to me I said, "Boy, I wish something would happen to you." He was so *mean*. Well, after my mother came home he came into the house and said, "See, Mother, I cut my thumb off." It was just hanging by the skin. He didn't even cry.

My mother grabbed her hair and run through the whole length of the house, screaming. Grandaddy was about two miles away doing some work in a neighbor's woods and she told me to go get him. I started running cross-country through all that snow, through the woods. I just knew my brother would bleed to death before I ever saw him again, and I bawled and I run through that snow all the way through the woods. Just before I got there I thought, "Now I'm going to shut up. I'm not going to be crying when I get there." Grandad saw me coming and hollered what was the matter, and I just whooped and fell all to pieces. By the time I got there Mother was there with the cutter; somebody had brought her by the road and she got there quick as I did. They had to call the doctor and he came clear out from Kalkaska, ten miles off. I guess there must have been a neighborhood phone somewhere. It was ten o'clock at night before he got to our place, and my brother was bleeding all that time. They never knew anything about tourniquets, and his thumb was still hanging. The doctor said he could fasten the thumb back on, but it would always bother him and be cold all the time, so he just took it off. He took the skin and pulled it over the stub. I felt bad for wishing something would happen to him, but my brother had more fun with that stub than anything. He'd put it up against his nose and make kids think he'd stuck his thumb up his nose.

That was the only time we ever had a doctor. If we got sick my mother would doctor us with skunk's oil and turpentine. Grandaddy would kill a skunk and she'd render it down and get the oil. She'd store that in a jar and then, when we'd get colds in the winter, she'd mix it up with turpentine and put it on our chests with a wool cloth over it. And if we got what they call the flu today, Mom would fix up onion syrup and goose grease for that. In summertime we got running of the bowels and she'd give us blackberry cordial. But she bought that. If there was any kind of sickness going around, my brother got it. He got mumps and he gave it to me. He got whooping cough and I got that too.

One time I remember we had a hole in the ceiling where we stored things. My uncle was up there handing down a flatiron to my mother and I was standing there looking up. The iron slipped and cut my head open. Mom sewed it up. With white silk thread. It didn't hurt much when she was sewing it because it was numb, I guess.

I've still got the scar. That's the way we did things.

There were quite a few kids around. I had a lot of friends. I had one Indian friend, a girl about my own age. She used to come to school and she'd come visit me. Those Indians back there were different, believe me. They were neat; they were big, stalwart people. I had a basket for years that she made for me, but I don't know what happened to it.

When we weren't in school or playing, us kids had jobs to do at home. Grandad and Uncle Nick would cut the wood, and my brother would have to pack it in. The chickens was my job. We had about fifty of them. Fed them in the morning and at night with our own corn. I don't know how many eggs they did lay, but we always had enough eggs to eat. It seems like my mother used to put them down in rock salt, but I wouldn't swear to that.

In the summer I had to pull weeds in the garden, and I had a little garden of my own, too. Grandad always gave me a little corner to myself. I'd grow what he did; he always gave me a few seeds of everything. I always had to do the dishes, that was my job, too. And my mother taught me how to hem and, believe me, I had to make those stitches just so or I had to take them out. She was strict. We didn't get too many lickings, but we used to get it sometimes. She got real mad one time and licked us with the buggy whip because we rode the horses and she told us not to.

My mother canned most of our food and put it down in crocks, in brine, in the cellar. She would make bags and stuff sausages in the bags and then hang them up out there in the hayloft to freeze through the winter. And in the winter, she'd sew or do different fancy work or make clothes and crochet. And of course, she did all the cooking. We'd have breakfast about six or seven—potatoes and side pork and eggs. And oatmeal. That was farm food. Grandad and my mother and my uncle had coffee in the morning. Us kids had milk. We had big meals at every meal. Noon, we'd have potatoes, vegetables, probably have pork, because we raised more pork than we did beef. Supper would be the same—potatoes, vegetables and meat.

They'd slaughter in the fall—I used to watch Grandad butcher the pigs—and it'd be cold enough in the winter to keep the meat. The coolest place we had was the root house; all the vegetables would be kept down there. It was dug down and then built over. The rutabagas and onions and carrots and potatoes would stay all through the winter. My grandad raised all of our own vegetables. We raised potatoes to sell so we could buy sugar and flour and that stuff; potatoes was our main source of income. We had to haul them into Kalkaska. And of course we had four or five cows and hogs and chickens. We had a barn which we kept nothing but hay in it, and we had a team of horses. We didn't have no steam-driven machines; we had horse-pulled plows, and a horse-pulled rake. Everything was with horses in those days.

One thing we didn't have to grow was berries, because they grew wild back there, raspberries and all like that—we went out and picked them up. Us kids would go in the woods and pick the raspberries and gooseberries, but Grandad always used to go to pick the blackberries. I don't know where he went, but he always gathered them for us.

Back there, farmers helped each other. Grandad did his own butchering, but some of the farmers would come and help him. Then he'd return the favor. And if somebody had a big hayfield, the others would help him out. The haying was done in July and August. Men would do one farm, then go on to another. The womenfolk would cook the meals for them. All the women came at haying time. And the kids would come over too, and we'd play and I'd probably have to wash the dishes. People weren't selfish in those days like they are today. Now it's everybody out for themselves, dog eat dog.

We had some good times back there. We had a lot of maple trees, and Grandad would draw the sap in the spring, and then we would have what they called socials. All the neighbors, the whole township, would draw sap from their own trees, and we'd all take it over to what they called the Grange Hall to cook it. We'd cook the sap down and make our own syrup and maple sugar. That was in the spring of the year, but there was still snow on the ground and of course us kids used to take a lot of syrup and make snow babies—you throw it out on the snow and eat it after it froze.

Sometimes we'd have box socials at the Hall. All the women would make fancy boxes with a lunch in it, have the box all fixed up pretty, and the men would bid on it. Of course a lot of them men knew which box was which. Sometimes they'd bid as high as ten dollars. All that was in wintertime, of course. In the summer everybody was too busy for that kind of thing.

At Christmas us kids got to go to town to do our own Christmas shopping. That was the only time we ever got to Kalkaska. We'd take the horses and sleigh, and we would heat up rocks and put them in the bottom of the sleigh around our feet so's to keep us warm. As far as I can remember we never had a tree. My brother would have one chair, and one chair was mine; when we'd get up in the morning our Christmas gifts would be on these chairs. And my Grandad would have gone out and tramped down the snow around the gateposts, and he'd put up corncobs on the posts. That's where Santa's reindeer had been to eat the corn. That was our way of celebrating Christmas.

I was always Grandad's favorite when I was a little girl. I remember one time he was going to go to town to the store, and he asked me what kind of candy I wanted. Well, the candy I liked was hoarhounds. Of course I got it wrong. First I said "the hoar candy" and then they started laughing at me, so I said "hound candy" and they laughed some more. But he brought me the candy. My grandad was pretty good to us kids. I didn't know anything about his folks. His mother was living in Hastings, I know, and I only saw her once when I was about ten years old, I think. She was the one that raised my mother. All I can remember is she was just elderly with gray hair. She had a beautiful home. I guess she must have been rich, because she lived in that nice house with her son, Ben. I only saw her that once.

I'm not close to my mother, never have been. It'll sound ornery, but I think it's because she was more wrapped up in my brother than me. He was the youngest, and a boy; that had something to do with it, I guess. But she's always been worrying about him and she didn't seem to worry much about me. She always called him her Sonny Boy, or Sonny Charlie. I was mud most of the time. But Grandad favored me, so I had a little bit of help.

One time—I was about ten years old, I guess—my mother sent me to Grand

Rapids to stay with her cousins. His name was Teunis Lambertson, if I remember right. I don't remember his wife's name because I didn't like her. She was mean to me. Teunis must have come up to see us and I guess he asked for me to come down. They wanted me to come down and help them, and Mom let me go. I stayed with them all one winter, didn't go to school. My mother's cousin was Christian, and his wife was Seventh Day Adventist. Her sabbath was from Friday night to Saturday night and his was on Sunday; so from Friday night to Sunday, nothing was done. We'd eat, but no washing the dishes or other work. Then I'd have all the dishes to do on Monday morning.

I didn't like it there. I got an abscessed tooth and an abscessed ear on the same side at the same time, and that woman would go away and leave me with all the dishes to do. I'd take the dishpan behind the little heating stove, put that side of my face to the heat and I'd wash the dishes and sit there and cry. That was an awful winter. That woman knew how miserable I was, but she didn't do anything about it, didn't take me to the doctor or nothing. Then his mother came down and she and I had to sleep together. One night my ear broke and she got up and took care of me; she babied me and made me feel better, but that didn't stop my tooth from hurting. It wasn't till Mom came down that I got to go to the dentist.

When I was only six years old my mother sent me down to my father's folks. She put me in charge of the train conductor and he was supposed to tell me what train to take in Grand Rapids, where I was supposed to transfer. But he never did. I just roamed around there in the station alone. I could have gotten on any cockeyed train. I could make out the Michigan Central because my mother had taught me a little spelling, so I got on that train and they could have taken me to Chicago for all I knew. But I got to my grandparents all right. My ticket showed Hastings, and the conductor put me off there. Such times kids go through!

I stayed with them about a year, didn't see my mother all that time. But I had a lot of fun. I had aunts and uncles my own age; one aunt was younger than me. We'd play, go down to the creek and set traps for muskrats. When my grandfather drove into town my grandmother would let us do anything we wanted to. We could tear the house down. There must have been six kids besides me. She had eleven or twelve all together; my father was her oldest. I went to school down there, had a really good time. Then my mother sent for me and I went back home. I don't think my brother ever went away.

When I was about thirteen Matt Aiken started to come by the house. Of course us kids was always hanging around him, and I guess that's what started it off with him and my mother. He was a good man, he was good to us kids. He and my mother went to Kalkaska one day and just got married. And then right after that he and Grandad came out here to Washington. When they got back home they said they wanted to come back out again, so Grandad sold the place, had an auction sale and sold the farm, all the livestock and farming tools. It was all sold. I don't know why they wanted to leave. They must have liked it better out here.

I wasn't crazy about leaving Michigan. But, then, I had to. I was just a kid—well, I wasn't so little, I was fourteen then, and sometimes I was sorry. Things were so different back there than it is out here. When we got out here it was just—oh, I can't explain it. Back there we had all the woods to play and roam in, and the places we used to go and gather wintergreen and the berries. They didn't have nothing like that out here. Here it was all desert. It was all different.

May: 1908-1929

When the Lambertsons arrived in Washington in 1908, May was fourteen. She was twenty-three and the mother of four daughters when the United States entered World War I. When the stock market crashed in 1929 and the country plunged into the Great Depression, she was thirty-five, a year away from being a grandmother. Some of the events of the twenty-one years between 1908 and 1929 May remembers clearly; others she remembers not at all.

Of World War I, May says simply: "We didn't want the Kaiser ruling the world. That's the way everything was told to me." The war made itself felt to the Lambertsons in the abundance of work available, and work took precedence over any ideological disputes.

In the influenza epidemic of 1918, half a million people died in forty-six states. May went daily into the open hospital wards to visit her brother, with no protection, not even a mask. She and Charlie were lucky enough to survive, but "people were dying like flies," she remembers.

Inflation followed the armistice, and the Lambertsons, like everyone else, had to pay almost twice as much for food as they had in 1914. And in the recession of 1921, when twenty thousand businesses failed and many industries cut the wages of their workers, the dressmaking shop where May worked went out of business.

During the years prior to and after the war, a strong radicalism manifested itself among the working class. In 1919 and 1920, a million workers were on strike and a million more were engaged in unrecognized strikes. Railroad workers demanded government control of the railroads; miners advocated nationalization of the mines. Official and unofficial response to the movement came swiftly. A Red scare swept the country: Attorney General A. Mitchell Palmer conducted countrywide raids, making mass arrests of political and labor leaders; individual states invoked criminal laws against radicals; newspaper headlines proclaimed the imminent arrival of Lenin and Trotsky; five duly elected Socialist members of the New York State Assembly were expelled as traitors; Sacco and Vanzetti were arrested for murder; the Ku Klux Klan, dormant for years, was reactivated and reached a membership estimated at four and a half million.

The state of Washington had a long tradition of radicalism. In 1896 a fusion ticket of Populists and reform Democrats had won the state election. In 1919, Seattle was shut down by a general strike organized by the AFL and the most radical of unions, the Industrial Workers of the World. To May and the other Lambertsons, the IWW was known as the I Won't Works. And sometime during the early 1920s, Matt Aiken joined the Ku Klux Klan.

When we first come out to Zillah it was November. It was apple time then; they were harvesting the fruit. For a while we all lived on a hillside just out of Zillah. Rented a house. Wasn't much of a house, not like it was back east. It was boards, not logs. Zillah was just a couple stores, a post office. Wasn't much. No streets. My uncle Nick started a shop, mending shoes, hand-sewing them. He always used to fix our shoes back east. And Grandad and Matt worked on the canal.

Then, later, Grandad and Nick got a house, and my mother and Matt and my brother got another house. I lived with Grandad and Nick. I done Grandad's housework.

I know I was sick all the time when we first got out here. I had a nosebleed. I'd wake up in the middle of the night with my pillow soaked. I don't remember being unhappy about being out here. Us kids was raised to be contented wherever our folks were. That was home and that was it. I went right into school and I met other kids. I was halfway through the ninth grade when I quit. I don't *know* why I quit. I always had a good time in school—used to think maybe I'd be a schoolteacher. My favorite subjects were arithmetic and physiology. I never did like history. Nor grammar. When I graduated from the eighth grade I had to take a state test and I passed high. I got ninety-eight for arithmetic. I don't know whether I had to go to work or what it was that I quit. I was fifteen then.

I went right to work for Mr. Granger, the head man of the canal. If I hadn't worked for him I guess I'd have worked on the ranches, thinning the fruit in the spring, when it formed, and going on to picking and packing. But I did all the housework for Mr. Granger—the cooking, the dishwashing, everything. They had six children and I helped take care of the baby, too. I remember I got four dollars a week and board; at night I'd go home to Grandad's.

Mr. Granger had a butler, a colored guy. When I wanted to go to a dance he'd do my work for me. I started going to dances then, when I was working out. A whole wagonload of us used to go out in the country to barn dances on Saturday night. There'd be a fiddler and we'd have food and dance. Sometimes we didn't get home till five in the morning, just in time to go to work.

I used to go to some rodeos over at Toppenish with this young fellow. His name was Fred Cox. I used to go with him quite a bit when I was young and foolish. I'd see the Indians then. They'd bring these horses in right off the range, wild ones. How they bucked!! And the Indians would ride them. Some of those Indian girls, they were really beautiful. But I never had anything to do with them; they never was in school with us. There used to be a little department store in Zillah and I'd hang around there. The woman that run it used to tell me to watch the Indians when they came in there, because they'd come in with those big blankets around them and shoplift.

A lot of the Indians worked in the hop fields in those days. I remember later, when I was married to Ernest, he worked for a meat market company and he used to go out to the hop fields, selling meat to them. I'd go with him once in a while. Those Indians didn't care what kind of meat they bought. It could be stinking and they'd still take it.

I guess I started thinking about getting married when I had a schoolmate that got married. I thought it'd be heaven, I guess. Wouldn't have to worry about anything. But when you get married you have more worries.

I worked all that winter for Mr. Granger. My stepdad kept telling me he needed my money and he'd take my check. And then in the spring I quit my job. I wanted to come over west of the mountains to visit my aunt who lived in Chehalis, and my stepdad gave me all my money that he'd saved for me. I stayed down with my aunt for a month and then I went back home and got married. I was sixteen. Dumb ox I was.

May: Michigan, ca. 1908

Ernest & May wedding photo 1910

His name was Ernest. Ernest Hochman. His brother had a livery stable down at Chehalis, and we had to get a horse and buggy to take us up to my aunt's. That's how I met him; it was Ernest who took us. Then he started coming around to my aunt's and we'd go to dances, things like that. When I came back to Zillah he came too and he ended up staying. He was good-looking, had curly hair. I guess that's why I married him.

My mother gave her consent, because I wasn't of age, and Ernest and me and my mother went over to Yakima and we got married by a justice of the peace. I remember I had a light blue dress. My aunt had it made for me by a dressmaker. It was long, to the floor, a kind of nice cotton material, not calico that they wore in those days. It had a high neck, long sleeves, tight waist. I had a waist in those days! Then, after, we went to stay with his folks; they had a farm about twenty miles away.

Oh gosh, I didn't learn about the facts of life till I got married. I'd kissed boys, but I didn't know nothing else. I knew how babies were born, but I didn't know how they got there in the first place. When I got my period I didn't know what that was. My mother told me it was just one of the things that happened; she didn't tell me what it was for. That part of marriage seemed like a duty, I guess. You get used to it.

My husband was a typical German. His folks came from Germany and Germans have their temper! Ernest'd just get mad at nothing, take it out on me sometimes. What used to get me is when we were sitting around with his folks, they'd all talk in German. I didn't know what they were saying. That used to get me down. I never asked them to talk in English. I was too mild and tender in those days, not like I am now. I took everything that was handed to me. I didn't have no backbone.

One thing I remember, my husband's father was a butcher, learned his trade in Germany. He could make the best blood sausage. With the blood sausage you had to catch the blood when you killed the animal and keep it stirred so it wouldn't coagulate. So I'd stand there stirring while he did the butchering. They slit the animal's throat and then hang it up to catch the blood in a bucket. That never bothered me, but, once, I tried to kill a chicken by cutting its head off. I missed and got the bill. I'd never do that again!

The year after we got married, we went back to Michigan. October of 1911 that was. Oh, was I pregnant! That was an awful ride going back there. Five days on the train, me big as a barn, feet all swelled up. We went back because my grandad and my brother went back there. I don't know why they went back. Gypsy, you know. And of course where my grandad was, *I* had to be. Mom didn't come till later; my uncle got malaria fever and she stayed in Zillah to take care of him.

When we got back there, Grandad had a farm down near Richland, in the southern part of Michigan. They weren't working the farm though. Anyhow, Grandad didn't know we was coming. We had to walk about five miles from the station and it was night when we got to the farm. We knocked on the door and Grandad pretty near—well, he didn't know *what* to think!

We stayed with Grandad all winter till Grace was born. I remember the day before she was born, I worked like a dog that day, getting the house all clean because I knew my mother and Matt and Uncle Nick was coming. I made pies, made bread, mopped the floor, got everything all nice. I guess it's because I knew Grace was on the

May:
1908-1929

127

way too. Then, when I went into labor, my uncle didn't know *what* was the matter with me. See, he was nothing but a walking skeleton from the malaria, and he thought I had got sick because I seen how terrible he looked.

My husband went for the doctor when I went into labor; it was about six miles away and the doctor come out to the house. Mom was there and she took care of me. Oh, I thought it was a hard birth, but I guess it wasn't. I remember how my brother said he wasn't going to have nothing to do with babies, but then he wanted to see it when it was born. My mother said, "I thought you wasn't going to have nothing to do with babies," and he said, "Well, this is different."

I named her Mary Grace. When I was a kid I read a book that had a girl named Grace in it, and I said to myself: "If I ever get married and have a baby, I'm going to call it Grace." I had a friend named Mary, so I named her Mary Grace, but I always called her Grace.

After she was born my husband went to work for these people and we moved into a house on their place. A lot of farms back there furnished a house for their workers. We got our vegetables and stuff off the farm he worked on, but we had to buy our own staples of course—sugar and flour and stuff like that. But we got our milk and butter from the farm too. We were there for about a year and then Ernest wanted to go back to his folks. When I wanted to come to mine, we did, so we went back to his. Coming back, I was pregnant with Annabel, so I was pregnant going and coming. My grandad used to say that the chickens got so used to moving that every once in a while they'd lay on their backs and stick their feet up in the air.

When we come back out here Ernest worked on his folks' farm for a while, and

May & Ernest: Zillah, ca. 1912

May on farm at Roy

Tacoma: 1920

May: ca. 1918

then he worked in the woods. He was working in the woods when Annabel was born. I didn't even have a doctor for her, just a midwife. My husband done so many odd jobs I couldn't keep up with him. And we kept moving around so much. Irene was born in Yakima; when I was carrying her we were picking fruit there. Then, after she was born, we moved to Tacoma and he was doing odd jobs in town. Then he worked in a lumber mill in Midland for a while, and then he quit that job and we moved back to Tacoma. He was always wanting to move. I hated moving! When we got back to Tacoma, we lived in what's the middle of downtown now. He was taking care of horses for the junk dealers. We lived there till Margaret was born in April of 1917.

So I had my four girls. I don't know what I'd have done if I'd had boys. Never wanted a boy, because my brother was so ornery to me. Figured all boys was that way.

After Margaret was born we moved out to Roy, about twenty miles out of Tacoma. Mom, Matt and Grandad had bought twenty acres of logged-off land out there. The menfolks built houses; we had just a two-room frame house, kitchen and bedroom. The kids all slept in one room, the rest of the house was kitchen. But we built a barn and we had a cow and a horse.

I saw Mom all the time then. She always helped me with the kids and we got on okay. In the evenings we'd take the folks' team of horses and hitch them up to the wagon and go out to a lake about six miles from the farm, fish for catfish—we'd all go, my mother and Matt and Grandad and the kids. It was all right out there, but we never did make a farm of that land. Matt was trying to, but him and Ernest had to work in the woods. They'd come back home on weekends and go back to the logging camp during the week.

Well yes, I remember the IWW then, but I don't know anything about it. I guess they were trying to make a union of the men who worked in the woods. I know Ernest never had anything to do with them. The men always said that IWW stood for I Won't Work. And I know they had that big massacre down in Centralia; the IWWs murdered some people down there, as far as I heard. I didn't know anything about it. I had four kids to worry about then. Unions wasn't so prominent as they are today. It was mostly just labor, not much union work.

Anyway, Ernest and Matt worked in the woods, and Grandad stayed home, just doing things around the place. We couldn't make a living off that place. We were just growing what we wanted to eat. So after about a year the chickens put their legs up again and we moved back to Tacoma. Brought the cow, Daisy, with us. She was too much of a baby to get rid of. She had wonderful milk. I used to roll her cream up and lift it off with a fork. Talk about cream!

My husband and I got along pretty good until that time. We were just like any family, I guess. I began to stick up for myself more, though. When Irene was a baby and we were living in Midland, he went out one night with a bunch of guys that he worked with at the lumber mill. He stayed out all night, playing cards and eating and drinking, I suppose. I got mad and I took the kids and got on the streetcar and went over to his folks'. That was on a Saturday night. The next Saturday night he was going to do the same thing. So I just got the kids ready and went with him. I stayed right there at that house where they played cards. I enjoyed myself; they had a nice feed and I had a good time too. He never did it again.

When he got ornery his mother would always stand by me. I never did confide in my mother. It would be like tattling on my family affairs. I just felt like: Why peddle everything? I'd rather go to his mother; it was *her* son.

One thing I remember about his folks is how, before the First War, when they sank the *Lusitania,* well, I guess everyone felt we ought to lick the Germans because we didn't want the Kaiser ruling the world. That's the way everything was told to me, so I thought the war was all right. Of course my husband's people were from Germany and they used to get into battles over that. His father would condemn the Kaiser, and his mother would stick up for him.

Things weren't bad during that war. There was quite a bit of work and my husband always had work when he wanted it; there was always odd jobs. That war ended when we were living in Tacoma. They had a big celebration, the town went wild, but it was a mistake; they thought the Armistice was signed, but it wasn't. Then a few days later the real end came. People were out on the streets, hollering and yelling and carrying on. Of course I didn't go, because I had four little kids to take care of.

It was after the war I started working out. My husband just stopped working. He started hanging around with that friend of his that had a lumberyard, and he'd stay away from home all the time, sleep at the people's house. I got sick and tired of it. That's when I began to stand on my own two feet. I had to go to work. Somebody had to work. He wasn't.

My first job, I went to work in a dressmaking shop in downtown Tacoma. In

May: 1920

those days you made designs of beads to put on the clothes—flowers, things like that. And then you'd have designs made of braid too. You'd have to put the flower pattern on the right side of the dress and do your beading work on it, and then you'd pull off the pattern. It was fascinating, all that kind of work. I really liked it. I worked there about six months until the dressmaker quit business. That was after the war, in the 1920s, I guess. A lot of businesses went under after the war, and the prices went way up too.

Ernest's not working—that was the whole size of it. I guess maybe we'd have gotten on all right if he'd worked. I *know* we would have. But I said, "If I have to work, I'm going to support my kids and myself. Not no man!" I wasn't going to support him *and* the kids. Never believed in that. If he was sick, that would have been different. Well, it had been leading up to it for about a year.

I never did tell my mother anything until the very last. Me and him got into an argument and he hit me. That was it. That's one thing I don't believe in—a man hitting a woman. They're so much stronger than a woman to begin with. I says, "I don't stay with no man who hits me," and I told him to get out.

That's when he went out and talked to my mother. He wanted her to talk me into taking him back. She came and talked to me, but in her heart I don't think she wanted me to take him back. She told him she'd ask, so she did. And I said, "No."

I was worried about how I'd get on, but then I went to work at the laundry down at the veterans' hospital and I got along all right. I remember I made sixty dollars a

May & Mutt: ca. 1922

month. I think I paid ten dollars a month rent, and I had to buy wood to cook and heat with, and there was electricity to pay. I worked ten hours a day, six days a week. There was no unions then.

I didn't know anything about Ernest after that. Not till afterwards. Then I found out he'd been seeing this other woman and he took her back east to Missouri with him. I didn't even *know* where Missouri was. That didn't bother me. I've always said that if they find somebody they like better than me, they can go. Ernest didn't live too long after we separated. He died of typhoid. His mother told my mother and she told me. I had got a divorce before he died. I had to sell my cow, Daisy, to pay for it.

As long as I had a job, nothing worried me. I liked work and I liked the money. I enjoyed the laundry, being around other people. I folded on the ironer and I worked on hand ironing. The ironers have big rollers you do the flatwork on. The other stuff has to be ironed by hand. Or they have the presses too, steel presses, just like a flatiron, that came down on top of the clothes. When I worked at the laundry at Fort Lewis, I ironed all the officers' shirts on those presses.

I remember I had long hair until I started working in the laundry. Dark brown—I wore it on top of my head. Then, after I had it all cut off, I wanted it back again. But I've never let it grow since.

My mother took the kids after we separated. I asked her to. They was alone all the time with me working. Sunday was the only day I had off. Mom and Matt and Grandad lived in Algona then and I'd go up there on my day off. I guess Grace was about eleven when they went to my mother. I can't keep track of exactly when these things happened. When they happened I'd try to get them out of my mind, and I don't try to remember anything about them.

I still had a feeling for my husband. Still do sometimes wonder about it. Stop and think about it. I think we'd have gotten on all right if he'd worked. I know we would have. But what could I do? I had to live. Kids had to eat.

May: 1929-1974

I met Mr. McCormack when I was working for that dressmaker in Tacoma; she was married to Mr. McCormack's partner. Me and Mrs. McCormack got to be good friends, but she died of cancer. I guess I started going with Mr. McCormack a couple, three years, after I got divorced. Mr. McCormack had a butcher shop in Olympia and he asked me to come and work for him, so I quit the laundry and went over there. I lived with Mr. McCormack's partner and his wife until me and Mr. McCormack got married. We went together quite a long time—about four, five years. Didn't get married until 1930.

Mr. McCormack was around forty-five when I married him; I was thirty-six. I always called him Mr. McCormack. His first name was Walter and people called him that, or Walt, but I never did. Don't know why. When I was talking to him directly I called him Jubie—that was a nickname a little kid gave him. But when I talked to someone else about him, I called him Mr. McCormack. He was a nice man. Different from my first husband. He didn't smoke, didn't drink. And he was always working. He was a lot neater than my first husband.

Grace and Annabel had come back to live with me when I went to Olympia. They went to school down there. I went to school too. Took up a course in bookkeeping at the business college, but I never followed it through. I kept the books in the butcher shop, but it made me too nervous to get a job anywheres else as a bookkeeper. I was always afraid I'd make a mistake. I'd rather sling sheets in a laundry; I knew how to do that. After a while I did go back to work in the laundry in Tacoma. I made more money there than I did in the butcher shop and I always felt a little independent when I had my own job. I didn't want somebody else supporting my kids, so I worked to take care of them as much as I could.

It's hard to say how I raised my kids. I tried to raise them right. So they didn't become streetwalkers anyhow. You know that song they used to sing—"I didn't raise my boy to be a soldier." You never know how your kids are going to turn out. I just raised them like anybody would, I guess. They went out with boys when they got old enough. I don't think I told them about sex, but they seemed to know. They all got married and they seemed to get along all right. Grace got married first. Her husband was in the Navy, and Grace stayed with me a little while—till her girl, Frances, was a pretty-good-sized kid. That was when we had the Depression, I remember. Then Grace went to work for somebody and took her kids with her.

Not many people had a job in those days. I remember in the butcher shop we were selling hamburger six pounds for a quarter. Steak was cheap, too. Liver, we gave away. We had Hoover then. I ought to remember him! A chicken in everybody's pot and two cars in the garage! But I had my job in the laundry, and Mr. McCormack kept the butcher shop for a while; we lost the shop in 1934. So many people were out of work. They'd charge their meat and couldn't pay for it, and we couldn't carry them anymore. When we closed the shop we had over four thousand dollars on the books. That was a lot of money in those days.

May: 1929

May & Walter: ca. 1942

Then Roosevelt took over. I think he was the first President I voted for. He brought in the WPA. Mr. McCormack worked for it for a little while, down on the wharf, doing some kind of bookkeeping; then he got a job at Western State Hospital as a butcher. We always had plenty during the Depression, but lots of people had to get their food through something like welfare is now. I might be a radical, but you can see that everytime there's a Republican in, it's the moneyed people that gets ahead. Poor people don't. It was Roosevelt who started the CCC camps, and that put a lot of men to work. Of course there was no businesses for a while. And they had to close down the banks, too. It wasn't till the war came that things got back to ordinary.

It's hard to say everything that happened in those years. Nothing special happened. Mr. McCormack and I got along all right. We had a house out by Steilacoom Lake. That's where I learned to swim. I'd wade out as far as I could and then swim back, so I'd know I wasn't in over my head.

When the Second War came we were living out at Steilacoom Lake. Mr. McCormack and his son-in-law was down fishing at the ocean front. Coming back home, they met all the Army trucks. They didn't know what was going on. I was home and had the radio on and I heard that Pearl Harbor was hit. That we were in the war. I was scared. We didn't know whether we'd be bombed over here. That was the worst fear. Then everything had to be blacked out at night; we had to put blankets over the windows so no lights would show out.

144   I remember they took all the Japanese that were out here and shipped them to the

Middle West. They had a lot of farms around here, grew vegetables to sell. The farms just went to pot since they shipped them out. We haven't had vegetables like that since. They were good gardeners, that's all I can say. A lot of these Japs they took away, I think they would have been for *us,* because they were American-born. But, still, you don't know what they would do, because the Japs were the ones who started with us, so they had to get them under control.

While the war was going on, it seemed like everything was ordinary. I had a cousin in it, but he came out all right. There was a lot of work, the shipyards were going and there was work out at Fort Lewis for civilians—that's where I worked at the laundry.

Grandad died during that war. That blow with Grandad was worse with me than with anybody. We were living out by the lake, didn't have a phone. Annabel called on my neighbor's phone. When I came to the phone, she said, "How are you feeling?" I said, "All right." She said, "Are you sure you're all right?" She just didn't know how to come out and tell me. Then she told me and it really broke me up. I had Grace's boy with me at the time so I couldn't go all to pieces, but that hurt me worse than anything. Grandad. I couldn't believe it. Sometimes yet I can hardly believe it. That he went like that. So quick. He was staying with Ruby and Charlie then. Ruby heard him moving around at six in the morning. At six-thirty he was gone. His heart. He was eighty-seven. They had the funeral in Yakima. It was during the war and you couldn't get gas, but Annabel had a friend who worked for the rationing board and she got us some coupons so we could get over there. That hurt me worse than anything.

May & Hannah: 1961

It wasn't long after that Roosevelt died. We owned a house outside Olympia and I was there, cleaning it up for renters, when the news came over the radio. Lord, I bawled like a cat. That was a terrible shock. I couldn't do any work, felt like the bottom had dropped out of everything.

Around the time Grandad died I'd just had an operation, so I quit work and stayed home for a year. Then a laundry asked me to fill in when one of their girls went on vacation. Well, that vacation never ended. Of course I was glad to have the job when Mr. McCormack died. He died in 1949. Of an ulcer. Never knew he had it. On Friday night he sat down at the table to eat and said he felt like he was going to faint, and he fainted. They gave him ten pints of blood at the hospital. Operated on him on Monday and they said the ulcer had gone clear through his stomach to his pancreas. The doctor said he had lost fifty percent of his blood before he ever got to the hospital. They operated on him on Monday, and on Tuesday he was feeling so good, I went back to work the next day. His daughter stayed with him on Wednesday, and when I got there after work he was in a coma. He died that night.

After Mr. McCormack died, I missed him, of course. But, then, I was working. I think when a person's working they're not as lonely as when they sit around home and dream about things. Married life's all right, but when you're older it don't pay to get married. You're set in your ways and he's set in his ways. When you're young, you're not so set. You grow together. I couldn't see getting married again after Mr. McCormack died. Now, Mom and Mr. Nesbitt, they were too set in their ways. I

May:
1929-1974

147

don't know if he didn't like me or what, but whenever I went over there he never talked to me. He'd go sit on the porch, say hello, and good-bye, but he wasn't sociable. He was a queer duck. I don't know how Mom got along with him. It's hard to say how she feels about things. She don't show feeling. When Matt died, she didn't show anything and I know she got along all right with Matt.

'Course I don't know anything about how she and my father got along. Only thing I remember my mother telling me is that he went down to his folks' after he left us and they kicked him out. I never saw my father again until 1959, I think it was. I'd gone back to Michigan to visit my aunts. My father was living in Battle Creek. He'd married again and one of his daughters wrote to me, and my aunt took me down there. He knew I was coming, so he knew who I was. Whether he would have known me otherwise, I don't know. I wouldn't have known him. We didn't do too much talking. My half sister done most of the talking. He could have been a stranger for all the feeling I had about him. He died a few years after that. He was ninety-three.

Things sure are different now from when I was young. We weren't dependent on nobody then. We had our food and our house. Taxes didn't amount to nothing in those days. We grew our own hay for the horses and cows. If you could just talk some of these young people into going on a farm, they would be independent. Your farms are laying idle around the country now. You can't get anyone to pick the berries. And there's the beans coming on and the rhubarb coming on and you can't get anyone to do the work. Maybe we weren't in silks and satins, but I think it was better than being on welfare.

A lot of people that you don't know about are living on welfare now. A family can make just as much on welfare as they would working. People aren't willing to work up to the top jobs. They want the top jobs to begin with. Well, no, I never did get any promotions myself, but bottom jobs are better than nothing.

We got freedom in this country to do what we want to do. Of course money talks. But I think if you're able to keep your head above water, and not be in debt to everybody, that's being successful. I never did think I'd have any money. Maybe if we hadn't lost the butcher shop, though, I'd have something today.

I'm living on my social security. Mom's on welfare, of course; when she was working out they didn't have any social security. I don't see her too much. I went to stay with her when she had that fall last year. I could live with her for a little bit, but I can't take a lot of it. I said to her, "Why don't you tell the welfare if you don't want to live alone. They'll have a woman come to stay with you." "I don't want nobody in my house," she said.

I wouldn't be surprised if she'd just go to sleep sometime and not get up. Which I hope does happen, I really do. Maybe it sounds hard, but I hope so. She says if we want to kill her, to put her in a nursing home. Grandad was eighty-seven when he died, so she's outlived him by a long ways. But I don't see how she can live much longer. She's gone downhill so fast. But you never know with these wiry old ladies. The U.S. would be two hundred years old the year she'd be a hundred.

I tried to be affectionate with my kids, more than my mother was. I don't remember her ever hugging or kissing me. My kids always said I favored Annabel, but I tried not to favor anybody. I don't favor *them,* but they treat me different. When

May & Felicia (Barbara's daughter), Jenny & Hannah: 1968

anybody's nice to you, you're different to them. Now Annabel, she's one of those people: You don't like my door, you don't have to swing on it! Independent. Irene is—I don't know how to say it—tenderhearted, I guess. Margaret's another independent one: You don't like me, you don't have to. Grace has got a very nervous disposition, very nervous temperament. I don't know why. I didn't think she was like that when she was a little girl, but maybe she was.

Grace

William Lambertson ———— Eleanor Ogden

Earl Barlow ———— Hannah   Nicholas

Ernest Hochman ———— May   Charles

Norm Peterson ———— Paul Owens ———— Grace   Annabel   Irene   Margaret

Bill   Frances

Barbara

Grace

There aren't many heirlooms in the Lambertson family. The artifacts of daily life were left behind, sold or lost as the family moved, easily replaced by more modern objects. But as the past became more precious than the present to Hannah, she distributed the few remaining family treasures that were hers. She gave one to Grace, together with a document of its authenticity. On a piece of paper Hannah wrote:

William E. Lambertson, great-grandfather of Grace Peterson, purchased this lamp, ready for the match, for the sum of 17 cents, in Hastings, Michigan, in August, 1901. Given to Grace Peterson by her grandmother, Hannah Lambertson Nesbitt, daughter of said William E. Lambertson.

Grandmother Hannah L. Nesbitt
Yakima, Washington, June 6, 1967

Aside from this kerosene lamp and a few other small links with her family's history—an amethyst ring made from a cuff link belonging to Hannah's grandmother; a knife with a staghorn handle, dated 1815, handed down to Hannah's father—Grace's three-room apartment, next door to a large shopping center on Tacoma's outskirts, is an anonymous place. Greenish-gray sculpted carpeting covers the floor of the small, square living room; two neon-bright prints of country scenes hang next to each other on the wall. The only signs of her personal life are graduation photographs of her two daughters, and one of Hannah, which flank the console color television set.

Grace is sixty-four and her health is bad. She looks haggard. Her voice is husky from too many cigarettes. She complains of almost constant pain in her left hand, which was injured at work, and she takes medication for a stomach ulcer. It is an unspoken but shared secret among the Lambertsons that she drinks.

Just before her first marriage, when she was not yet eighteen, Grace was a round-faced, plumply pretty girl. A year or two later the baby fat melted and she became a beautiful woman—taller than her mother and grandmother, slim, high-cheekboned. In her later twenties she grew even thinner; her skin stretched tightly across the bones of her face, and she had the classic looks of Appalachian Mountain women, so gauntly beautiful in youth before they become suddenly careworn in their thirties. Of the Lambertson women—all of them good-looking—she was the most beautiful and she is the most bitter. Perhaps, being beautiful, she felt life owed her more; or the time in which she grew to adulthood—the postwar 1920s, with its flappers, flouting of Prohibition, open representation of sex in movies and magazines—promised perpetual excitement. Whatever it was life seemed to promise her, it did not deliver. "Mom always had a dream," her daughter Barbara says. "I don't know what it was. I don't think she knew what it was. But she never, ever could find it." At the very least a dream must be named to make it come true.

Grace has been married three times. Her first husband deserted her and their two children. She can speak of him now only as "he." She left her second husband, Barbara's father. She can say no more about that marriage than "It went sour." And mention of her third marriage draws this response: "The less said about that one, the better. I don't even think about it anymore. As far as I'm concerned, it's just something that didn't happen."

There are many things in her life that she would like to believe didn't happen, and that she won't talk about with anyone. I know how much she hasn't said, and what she has glossed over, because her daughter has been an observer of her life and has told me the facts as she saw them. If Grace refuses to acknowledge them, I think it is because they make no sense to her. She reaches for explanations that sound lame in her own ears. And much of what has happened fills her with shame. She has felt desperation too often, and, in desperation, has left people and places, going toward what she never could say except that she wanted a "change." The aimless movement, the dream without a name, the things that didn't happen, have given her an ulcer, frequent insomnia and a need for alcohol and tranquilizers.

Grace: 1911-1929

I know I was born in Ross Township, Michigan, in 1911, and they brought me out to Zillah when I was a year old. But I barely remember anything about Zillah. I remember when we moved over here to Tacoma they brought me on a train, and Grandaddy bought me white gloves that came to my elbows.

How long we lived in Tacoma, I don't know, but then we moved out by Roy. Mom and Dad, my uncle Charlie and Grandma and Grandpa Matt, and Grandaddy had acreage out there. Grandpa Matt worked in the woods and I guess my dad did too. I didn't start school till we moved back to Tacoma from Roy. I don't know why we moved back. My father was always moving.

There were all four of us kids by then. I'm the oldest, then Annabel, Irene and Margaret. Margaret's the only one I remember being born. I remember my father taking me and Irene over to a neighbor's house with our breakfast because Mom was having Margaret.

My father was tall, blond-haired. One time when we lived on Ninety-sixth he took me with him to call on another woman. I was about six then. I just sat there while he talked to her. I remember he had his legs crossed.

He beat Mom a lot. I saw it. He was cruel to our cow too. He kicked it. One time I shut a window on Irene's finger and he beat me with a piece of stove wood. He was always beating us kids. Especially me. Mom would try to interfere, but it didn't

159

do any good. He'd beat her too and she'd cry. Mom'd go to Grandma's, and then Dad would have Grandma talk her into coming back. The last time he beat Mom, Grandma wouldn't talk her into it, because she'd seen the bruises he put on Mom. Mom must have told my father to go then. She'd had to go to work to support us anyway. He never could keep a job. It's funny, but I know we missed him when he left.

We lived with Mom for a few years after he left. She was working all the time, but I remember there was one summer when she kept all of us kids in white clothes; we had clean, white dresses every day. During school I'd come home at lunchtime and fix lunch for the two younger kids and then go back to school. Irene and Margaret would be by themselves, but they were good; they'd play in the house or in the yard all day. But then we all went to live with Grandma in Algona. I was about eleven then. I remember I had long blond hair and that summer I cut it. It was the first time it had ever been cut. Before that, my aunt Agnes used to put it up in rags to make those sausage curls.

Mom paid Grandma for our room and board, and we made extra money in the berry fields. On weekends, and after school in the fall, and when we didn't go to visit Mom in the summer, Grandma and Grandaddy and us kids would pick berries in Lockridge's fields. You got paid by the crate and we used that money to buy material for our clothes.

Grandma taught me how to sew and knit and crochet. And I can remember Grandma and Grandad teaching us our ABCs. And arithmetic. Grandad taught us how to figure. He was good at that. He could figure things out in his head faster than we could on paper. After I learned how to read I had to read to Grandpa Matt. He never went to school and didn't know how. I had to read to him till I was hoarse. He liked westerns, Zane Grey books. I didn't like them too much, but I had to read all of them to him.

Grandma was strict with us kids, believe me. She taught us to do things around the house, but I had already learned those things for myself when Mom was working. I was the oldest, so I was more or less responsible for the others. We went to the Pentecostal Church a couple of times a week, and we never missed a Sunday unless we were sick. Grandma was strict about everything. We couldn't have kids come in and play with us, and we couldn't go out and play with anyone. We could play with the kids at school, but that's the only time we got to play with anybody outside ourselves. We couldn't play cards. We couldn't even *look* at a deck of cards.

It was only a three-room house Grandma had in Algona. Annabel and I had to fix up the attic to sleep in. There was a door that opened into it and we'd let the air in that way. No windows.

I remember downstairs Grandad's chair was right by the stove, with just a passageway to get to the bedroom. It was an oak rocking chair and he'd sit in it all the time. Grandad used to chew tobacco and spit it into the bucket. He'd get it in, but he always managed to splatter too, and I'd have to wash it up. There wasn't running water; you had to get it from the well. We had kerosene light for a while and then they got what they called gas pipes. You had to pump them up.

161

Grandma had a lot of work to do: washing, mending, ironing. She had to wash on an old washing board. She'd boil the clothes on the stove in a big copper boiler that she used for canning, too, and then scrub them on the board. Washing was an all-day job. She had clothes to wash for us four girls, two men and herself. She was always busy. I did the ironing for her. We had three flatirons. You heated them on the stove and you put the cold one behind and took the front one. Sometimes Annabel ironed, but she wouldn't stick to it. She didn't want to work. One time Grandma made me iron so long—just to see how long I'd stand there and do it. She didn't apologize then, but later she said she was ashamed of herself.

Grandpa Matt was working in the woods then, peeling poles. He peeled the bark off cut trees. We used to go with him once in a while. We'd go in his Model T and spend the day in the woods while he was working. There were a couple of deer up there and he used to take cake for them in his lunch. Grandpa Matt worked in the woods every day till he had his stroke. I guess I was about fifteen then. I remember he got up one morning to build the fire, got the fire half laid and then he fell across the stove. Grandma called us and Grandad and then they called the doctor. Matt lived a long time after that, but he was paralyzed. He never had any use for his right arm, and he couldn't work.

I guess the only money Grandma had after that was what Mom gave them for our board. And what we made picking berries. There wasn't any welfare then and no unions at all in them days. The men in our family never had anything to do with unions. I remember there was a bunch of the I Won't Works, and they'd march and have parades and carry signs and stuff. But all the men in our family worked in the woods and never talked about it or complained. It was just outdoor work.

I do know that Grandpa Matt belonged to the Ku Klux Klan. It was very secret. Grandma told us about it later. I don't know anything about it. It was just a secret organization like your Elks or something. It was a club, and you're not supposed to tell anything about the doings in your club. I never seen any of that burning crosses in yards and stuff up here. We never had any trouble like that.

Of course grown-ups didn't talk to kids about things like that. Us kids just talked amongst ourselves, and grown-ups talked grown-up talk. You didn't talk to grown-ups unless you wanted something. I can remember Grandpa Matt having a crystal set and I'd listen to it, so I found out some things about what grown-ups thought. Like a lot of people admired Lindbergh. I heard about him. And Coolidge. But all us kids knew about was going to school and going to church.

One Sunday, Grandma took us to church up in Auburn. I guess we went there to see Grandma Hochman, my dad's mother. That's when she told us that our father had passed away. I felt sad, I remember that. I hadn't seen him in years; I was about eight when he left, and about fifteen when he died. I didn't cry. None of us kids did. But we did feel bad about it 'cause it was our dad. I don't remember Mom or Grandma saying anything to us about him. About where he went when he left us or about his dying. If they did, I don't remember. Our family was pretty reserved. We didn't talk about things like that. We never were an affectionate family. Grandma wasn't affectionate; neither was Matt or Mom. Only thing they let us know was when we did something wrong. We'd get punished for it. Spanked. Or we'd have to sit in a chair and not talk to anybody for a while. I never got any hugging or kissing. Grandaddy used to hold us on his lap once in a while when we were little. He had a good education. And Grandma and Grandpa Hochman were always affectionate, but of course we weren't around them too much. I guess that's how I learned to be so darned independent. Don't take nothing from nobody. But as far as I can remember I've been nervous all my life. When I was little I couldn't stand to have anybody around when I was nervous. I'd just sit with my nose in a book and not talk to anybody.

We stayed with Grandma until Mom started working for Mr. McCormack in the butcher shop. Then I went down to Olympia to live with Mom. Later Annabel came down and lived with us, and then, after that, Irene came; but she lived with the preacher's family as a mother's helper. At first we all lived with Mr. Jackson and his wife, Mildred—Mr. McCormack's partner. Then Mom and Mr. McCormack got married. We all knew they were going to get married. I don't know why they waited so long. I liked Mr. McCormack. He was a very dignified and clean man. Even his fingernails were always clean. He was good to us kids. In the summers we'd go fishing and camping together, hike in the woods. He never hit us. Never had a cross word for us either.

I started working in the butcher shop while I was still in school. I made hamburger and link sausages; you'd put the sausage meat in a machine, and the skin would come out on this little arm. The meat would fill the skin and you'd twist the skin every so often. I got paid for it, but it went mostly for my room and board.

Annabel and I quit high school at the same time—my first year of high, when I was sixteen. In a way I was glad to leave school. I used to play hooky to work in the butcher shop, and Mom would write me an excuse to get back into study hall. We'd do that all the time. But, in a way, I wasn't glad either. I was best in math, always liked it. I'm still good at it. I liked geography too. I don't really know why I quit.

When Mom moved back to Tacoma to work in the laundry, we went with her. Annabel and I didn't do much of anything in Tacoma. Didn't get jobs or anything. We'd walk over to Wright Park and walk home. Sometimes the kids we knew in Olympia would come up and we'd go to movies at the old Pantages Theatre down on Ninth and Broadway. In those days there were ballrooms and we'd go to dances. There was one on Ninth and Pacific and another on Eleventh and Market. You'd pay to get in and there were always sailors to dance with.

One time Annabel and I went to a dance and there were a bunch of sailors from a ship that had just got to town. We danced with two of them. Mine's name was Paul Owens; Annabel's was Bob. Then we went back to the ballroom another time and met them again. They took Annabel and me home and the four of us started going out together. We'd go to dances and to shows, or we'd go out to Point Defiance or fool around at home playing cards and things. He asked me to marry him right away, a few nights after we met. I told him no, but I ended up marrying him anyway, so I might as well have said yes the first time.

It's hard to say what he was like. He was kind of quiet. Angular face. Black curly hair. A little bit taller than I am. He was all right. He was from Virginia; I never met his folks. We got married before his ship pulled out. I guess that was a couple of months after I met him. I was almost eighteen.

I was happy about getting married. A little bit scared, but happy. I thought I loved him. Mom liked him. She had to give her consent, because I wasn't quite eighteen.

Mom and I have never been close, really close. To be honest, my sister Annabel was always her favorite. I was more or less shoved to the side. And Margaret was always Grandma's favorite. So Irene and I always felt like outcasts. We've always gotten along good together, Irene and me.

Grace was married in 1929, just before the stock market crash and the beginning of the Great Depression. "Hard times, awful times," Hannah called it. But there had been hard times before for the Lambertsons. Life on the edge of the economy had never been easy, and they didn't have much to lose. Even in the relative prosperity before the crash, sixty percent of Americans had incomes below two thousand dollars a year, the minimum amount estimated as necessary for basic necessities.

The early years of the Depression had little effect on Grace, whose husband was paid regularly by the Navy. But in 1932 and 1933, she felt its full impact for a time.

To millions of Americans, including the Lambertsons, Franklin Roosevelt was to be the saviour, inspiring the same faith John Kennedy would thirty years later. Roosevelt's administration, with its host of agencies—CCC, TVA, NIRA, WPA, NRA—had some effect on reducing unemployment: from its peak of fifteen million, unemployment dropped to about ten million and remained there all through the 1930s. To the political right and to business, the growing power of the Federal Government was an anathema; to the left its programs were palliatives. All through those terrible years when respectable people scavenged for food in garbage cans, when the dust bowl made migrants of thousands of farm families, the promise was that "prosperity is just around the corner." It was a promise that was not fulfilled until World War II erupted in Europe and war orders poured into American factories.

Grace:
1911-1929

Grace: 1929-1974

I got married the last of August 1929 in a church in Tacoma. There was just Mom and Annabel and Paul's friend Bob. I had a dress that I made for the wedding. It was kind of a beige color, figured, with a big lace collar, full skirt to the middle of my knees.

After the ceremony Annabel and Bob and us went out to eat at some big restaurant downtown, which isn't there anymore. Then we went to a hotel room and stayed there for a couple of weeks till his ship left. Mom didn't tell me anything about what to expect. I knew, because we kids had talked about it. But I didn't know anything about babies. I didn't know where babies came from. One time when we were living on Roosevelt Heights I was sleeping with Mom. She had her period and it got on her nightgown. She said, "One day you'll be like this, too." I knew about the period from kids at school, but I didn't know what it meant. I just knew I was going to have it. The night I got married I was scared. It was painful. But I got to enjoy it.

He was on his first or second turn in the Navy when I met him. His ship would go from Tacoma to San Pedro, then down to the Panama Canal, then over to the Hawaiian Islands. On maneuvers, they called it. When it went to the Canal or the Islands, he'd be gone for a month or two. After we got married his ship went down south to San Pedro, so I went to Los Angeles by bus and then I took the electric car to Long Beach. We had an apartment there, right on the beach. It was a nice little place, had one of those wall beds and a little kitchenette, a little false fireplace with a gas burner in it if you needed heat. When the ship was in San Pedro he came home when he didn't have the duty—about every other night and every other weekend.

He was a quiet guy, didn't have too much to say. I had a couple of girl friends from Algona who were married to sailors and living down there, too. We'd get together during the day. They'd come over, or we'd walk uptown, go to the amusement park. When our husbands weren't in we'd go up to the boardwalk in the evenings where they had a dance hall. The guys would have to pay ten cents a dance to dance with us. We had a lot of fun. There was a theater there and every week they put on a different show. And we'd go to the beach. When my husband was home we'd stay home at night or go up on the pier or have a beach picnic. His friend Bob had a girl and we'd all go out together. I was having a good time. Even when he was gone a month or two I was never lonely, always had friends to talk to, run around with. I knew it was the Depression then, but it never bothered me at all, because he had a steady income from the Navy.

I stayed in Long Beach till the next summer, when his ship came back up to Tacoma on summertime maneuvers, and I lived with Mom until before Bill was born. That was in October 1930.

My husband was surprised at how much I didn't know. He told me about babies. I didn't know anything about birth control, but he did. But we wanted a baby, so when I got pregnant he was happy about it and so was I. I was with Mom the summer I was pregnant, and then I went down to Long Beach to have the baby at a hospital with a Navy doctor. The Navy paid for everything. Then when I came home my husband took two weeks' leave to help me. I named him William after Grandad, but I always called him Bill or Billy. And of course I knew how to take care of babies because I had so many sisters.

After I had the baby I couldn't go out so much as before, but my friends and I would take the baby down to the beach. By this time the girls I'd gone to school with in Algona were gone; their husbands had been transferred. But I knew another girl, and sometimes she'd take the baby even when I didn't have to go anywhere. She was crazy about him.

I loved my husband when I married him. And for a long time afterwards too. Till he deserted me and the kids. He started being mean to me before I got pregnant with Bill. After Bill was born he was pretty good, but then he started again and it kept getting worse. He'd just haul off and hit me. Over nothing. He didn't use his fist, just his open hand, but I got tired of it and didn't care anymore. He'd come home and start arguing about anything—over something I hadn't done or something he thought I had done. Just pick an argument. I'd argue back and that's when he'd hit me. I was too mad to cry; I'd just walk out of the house, walk around the block.

When Bill was about eight months old we came back up to Tacoma because my husband's ship came up. I got pregnant with Frances then. I didn't want to get pregnant, and my husband didn't want a second baby, but he didn't try to do anything about it. And I didn't know what to take.

Frances was born at Mom's in April 1932. My husband was down at Long Beach. I hadn't seen him for a while. We didn't have the apartment in Long Beach anymore, because he didn't want us to come back down there. He wanted us to stay in Tacoma.

When Frances was born he paid for a doctor to come to the house, and then he came up, but he didn't stay. Then it got to the point where he wouldn't send me any money. I wrote to his commanding officer about it, and he made my husband give me an allotment. It was ninety-two dollars a month, and that was a lot of money in those days. That's when my husband deserted the Navy. He jumped ship in San Francisco. First his commanding officer wrote me a letter saying he was away without leave. Then I got a notice from Washington, D.C., saying he'd deserted. After that my allotment stopped.

Mom never asked me anything about what was going on, and I never told her. I talked to Annabel, told her about how mean he was to me. One time she was there when he said something mean to me, and she hit him in the face. Bob was there and he took him out of the house. Later Bob told me my husband was going around with other women when I wasn't around.

Frances was about a year old when he deserted. I'd left Mom's and was living with Grandma, Uncle Charlie and Grandad in Auburn. Grandpa Matt was dead. We lived on Uncle Charlie's pension—he got that from his insurance policy when he got crippled with arthritis—and what we made picking berries. Then I got a job with some guy across the Bay, keeping house for him and his twins. I had Bill and Frances with me, so I had four kids to take care of. This was 1933. You couldn't get jobs then, and I had to stop working for this guy because he wanted me to go to bed with him. I wasn't about to do something like that.

I moved out of his house into a place of my own, just a two-room shack by the railroad tracks. It had a garage I used as a woodshed, a cookstove, indoor water, but we had an outhouse. The Red Cross helped me. They gave me wood and vouchers for food, but it wasn't enough. I didn't go back to Grandma's because she had enough to do taking care of Grandad and Uncle Charlie. Grandma knew a man from church who worked in a restaurant. He'd bring the leftover food to Grandma, and Grandaddy would bring it down to me.

The Red Cross helped whoever they could. There wasn't any welfare then. Just WPA and I couldn't get a job on that. That was just for men. There weren't any jobs to be had. There were a lot of people suffering. I seen breadlines in Tacoma and in Auburn. People scavenging in garbage cans in the backs of restaurants, trying to find something to eat. So many people were destitute. Lot of people wouldn't have had anything to eat if they didn't have places where they could raise a little garden. In Algona, in the valley, that's what everybody did. And they'd pick berries in the summer. You didn't get much for them, but every little bit helped. I took Bill into the berry fields with me when I picked. He'd sleep under a gunnysack in the shade, and I had a schoolgirl who came out and took care of Frances.

Then I started going with Norm Peterson, Barbara's dad. I'd known him from school in Algona. We met again when I moved to Auburn. Norm's mother had a cow and she used to give me milk, and vegetables from her garden. Norm had work. He was one of the lucky few. He was driving a truck hauling four-foot timbers for his brother-in-law, Jack. Jack had a fruit stand, and Norm would go to Yakima and bring back fruit and timber. I guess Jack sold it to the Red Cross. Norm always worked during the Depression. None of our family really suffered. The hardest time I had was before I married Norm.

I got a divorce from my first husband. On grounds of desertion. All you had to do was put an ad in the paper for six weeks, and you could get a divorce. Norm and I got married in 1933. Barbara was born in 1934. We lived in Auburn till Norm got a job on the railroad in Yakima, and then we all moved there—that was around 1936. Norm was a welder and a wrecking engineer. Whenever there was a train wreck, they'd get out the wrecking crew; and he welded the box cars and engines whenever they needed welding.

I liked Yakima. We had a big house, with a washing machine, those wringer types. Later on, we got some nice furniture from Montgomery Ward and Sears. We were always moving, though. We lived in lots of different houses.

I wasn't working then. Once a week my friend Edith and I would take Barbara—Bobby, I called her—to a show; we took her to every one of the Shirley Temple movies. Bobby wouldn't let anyone say a word when the movie was on. We'd go to a matinee and then go shopping afterwards. On the weekends we'd all go fishing and camping in the summer. And then, in August, we'd go out to pick hops. Bobby was too young, but me and Bill and Fran picked. Everybody who didn't have steady work picked hops. Now it's all done by machines, but then it was all picked by hand. You wore gloves, cut the vines and stripped the hops into a basket. The hops are all in a cluster and you had this big pole—it looked like a scythe—and you reach up and cut the vines and strip them into your basket. We'd start early in the morning, the earlier

Norm & Grace, Fran,
Barbara, Billy: 1938

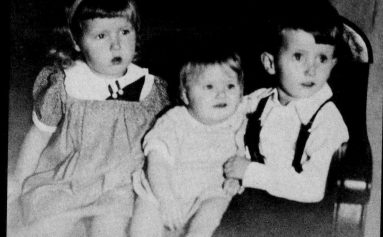

Fran,
Barbara,
Billy: 1935

the better. Later it got too hot to work. We'd start around seven and quit at two, depending on the heat. You could pick eight hundred pounds a day if you were fast enough. You got paid by the pound, and a person could average fifteen or twenty dollars a day. Fran could do that; you had to jump to keep up with her.

My kids were all different from each other. Bobby was always a reader. Always had her nose in a book. She'd read anything she could get her hands on. Fran liked her dogs and she liked sewing. Billy didn't want to read or anything else. He liked model airplanes and stuff like that. He was a small child; he's still small. I took him out of the town school because the principal there implied he was a dummy; she said he couldn't learn. But I put him in another school and he was perfect. He always did his studying. There was nothing wrong with that boy. He always had to prove himself when he was growing up, because he was so small. One time he came home—he had this maroon sweater on—and he took it off and his shirt was covered with blood. "That blood don't belong to me, Mom," he said. He just had to prove himself with his fists. Sometimes Billy and Fran would ask me about their father. I just told them he was gone. I couldn't tell them anything else. I didn't know anything else.

Norm was real good to Billy and Fran. And Bobby and her dad were real close. He always called her "Joe," for Joe Palooka; I called her "Babe" 'cause she was the baby of the family. Norm and I got along all right for a while. We had a good marriage for a long time. It just went sour. *I* don't know why. Well, we were always in debt. He'd mortgage the furniture to buy a car, then get finished paying that off and want to buy another car. We were always arguing about money. That was the big problem, I guess.

Not too much of anything else, just that mostly. It started to go sour before Bobby went to school. He never hit me or anything. He threatened to once. Grabbed me and pushed me into the cabinets. I had my hand behind me and there was a butcher knife there. I picked it up and said, "Let loose of me or I'll cut you." And he never tried to touch me again.

But he wanted things his way. He'd always say things like, "We do what I want to do or else we don't do anything." Like sometimes I'd want to go for a ride and he wouldn't. We argued about things like that. He wouldn't talk about things. If we had a fight he'd just go outside. I stayed with him because I didn't want to break up Bobby and her dad. And we'd go out and have a good time sometimes. Go fishing and camping. Norm didn't like to dance, though. I always did. I don't know why it went sour.

When the war came, I was at home making clothes for the kids' dolls for Christmas when I heard about Pearl Harbor. I put the radio on, and at first I just thought it was part of the program they had on. Then I realized. From then on we'd hear about the Germans bombing England. But it wasn't like it is now. TV brings everything more home to you because you see the conditions. What really brought it home to us was when Norm's sister's boy got killed. He was killed on Iwo Jima just before they raised the flag. That really brought it home.

Grandaddy died during the war, too. Grandma had moved over to Yakima by that time and we'd go out and see her at least once a week. We went over there the night before Grandad died. Norm's boss had bought us a case of beer and we took

Grace & May (far right) with women from laundry, 1946

some over there. Grandad had a bottle of it. I've always felt bad about that, and yet I didn't. He enjoyed it. That's the last time I saw him alive. He died the next day in Grandma's arms. He'd always lived with Grandma, came west with her, went back east with them all when I was born. She was holding him when he died.

A few years after the war started we moved back to Tacoma because Norm got a job on the railroad there. We lived in this project; it was brand new, built for defense workers at the shipyards and Army and Navy personnel. That's when I went back to work. I'd rather have been home taking care of my youngsters, but I had to work because we were always in debt. Norm'd brag: "Well, I finally got the old woman to working." From that time on I've always worked. Bobby was about nine or ten by then.

I'd get the kids up in the morning, and they were old enough to get back and forth to school by themselves. Bill had a paper route in the evenings. He'd iron his own clothes if I didn't have the time. I worked in the laundry with Mom. I was a folder and a flat-work ironer. Helping fold sheets, pillowcases, napkins, whatever came through the ironer hot. Mom was a stacker. A stacker ties everything up in bundles and puts the right name on it.

When we went back to Yakima after the war, I worked in the laundry there. I was the head folder for a while, then the stacker and pricer. I had to make out the bills for doctors, hotels, motels. The head folder is responsible for how everything looks. I loved my work. It was interesting. It was both physical and mental because I had so much pricing to do. You never knew when the prices were going to change and you'd have to start memorizing all over again. You had to know what everything cost—a pair of pants, a man's shorts, a shirt, pillow slips, sheets. You get a bundle from one family, and the marker counts it all up and sees what's in it. Then the pricer prices it. When I was pricing I'd price the fancy stuff. Like a tablecloth has to be priced by the size, or if it's lace. And the fancy dresses, if they have ruffles that had to be ironed. And men's tuxedoes, if they have frills down the front, fancy bedspreads with ruffles—all those had to be ironed by hand.

You got to recognize the clothes a lot of times. We had one man, he always left money in his shirt pocket. And one man invariably left his watch and snuff in his pants pocket. When you got his bundle you knew you'd better look. In overalls you were always finding wrenches and stuff like that. And cufflinks in shirts. One time I found a wedding ring in a uniform pocket. It was fun just to see what you could find.

I went on my own in 1949, I think it was. Well, I just couldn't take it anymore, always being in debt. Sometimes my whole check went to pay off our debts. The kids were big enough to take care of themselves. Bill was in the Navy; he joined when he was seventeen. And Fran was living with some people as a mother's helper. Bobby was the only one at home and she was working parttime. So I decided I'd had enough of it. I know Bobby didn't like it when I left. But she was just a kid; when you get older you see both sides of it.

Norm was real upset. Well, he acted belligerent. He was a belligerent man. He just tried to see how much of a hard time he could give me. Oh, he did little things to make it rough for me. He said I'd taken Fran's baby shoes that I'd had bronzed; he was going to have me thrown in jail for that. Well, I *hadn't* taken them. And he went through my trunk, which he had no business doing. It wasn't his, it was mine!

I moved to a little apartment in Yakima. My kids were all right. Fran got married and I gave her a church wedding in the big Catholic church; she became a Catholic before she married Jim. I liked Jim. He and Fran had been planning to get married since they were in high school together. Jim's one who's never out of a job. He worked in the orchards for his brother-in-law; then he and Fran moved to Tacoma and he got a job with the railroad for a while.

By the time I left Yakima, Bobby had a little apartment of her own. Well, I just wanted to get away for a while, so I came over here to Tacoma on a vacation and went down to the laundry where Mom was working. Nan, the boss, says, "When are you coming back to work for me?" So I said, "Give me enough time to go back over there and give my notice." I stayed with Mom a couple of months, and while I was there Bobby came over and stayed with us for a week until she and Ed got married. After that I moved to Bremerton and worked in a laundry over there. I got married again.

I don't want to talk about him. I really don't like him. *Everything* was the matter with him. After I got to know him. Before he was all right. He's got a wonderful family. His name was Ralph. I met him in Yakima. He was living in the same apartments I was, and the landlady introduced us. He was just a big baby. Looking for a mother character, I guess.

We got married in 1952 and lived together a couple, three years. He was a cook when I met him; when we went to Bremerton he worked in the Navy shipyards. He was always gone somewhere. Once Bobby brought Lisa up to see me for a visit; Lisa was just a little girl, could hardly talk, and she looked up at me and said, "Don't your man live with you no more?" That time he was supposed to be out hunting with some guy. I found out later he took a woman with him.

After I left him he kept bothering me. One time he tried to climb in the window of the laundry. The boss said that if he tried that again, he'd have him arrested. I'm so nervous anyway, I just couldn't stand it. I married because I was lonesome and I was glad to be out from under when that marriage broke up. The less said about that one, the better. I don't even think about it anymore. It's just something that didn't happen.

After that, I was very happy. I had a lot of friends in Bremerton and we went places. I worked all day, and at night I'd have company or I'd be at somebody's place visiting. On the weekends a whole gang of us used to travel all over the state and go down to Oregon. I didn't have time to be lonely.

Then Bobby called me; she was divorced from Ed and was married to Carl Eccles and living over in Yakima. And she said the laundry there was looking for a checker and would I take the job. I wanted to get out of Bremerton. I wanted a change of scenery, I guess. So I went back over there and made all new friends. The friends I used to have were all married couples, and they don't have room for a third party. I made single friends, and the girls and I used to go out and have a ball. We'd go dancing, do different things. I stayed there until I got my hand hurt in the laundry. I haven't worked since July of 1970.

When that accident happened I was a checker and the head of the finish department. I had to check the finished stuff out, and I was trying to get some coveralls untangled because they were all twisted when they came out of the extractor.

It tore the tendons in my wrist. At first the doctor thought it was a sprain, but it didn't get any better. Then another doctor put a metal splint on it. I kept on working, but it was hard. Then I had an operation and physical therapy and a cast and another operation. I've had four operations. After the last one the doctor came in and said he'd never seen such a mess as my hand. It was full of tumors. I said, "You thought I was kidding, didn't you?" And he said, "Yes." I guess he thought I just wanted to keep on collecting money from the state. I was getting State Industrial Insurance.

After I had to stop working I stayed with Uncle Charlie and Aunt Ruby. I wasn't getting enough money to keep up a place of my own. But then I wanted to get out of Yakima, so I moved back over here to Tacoma. The benefits are higher here, and rent's cheaper because I got this apartment through the housing authority; the government pays the difference between what I can pay and what my landlord charges. That landlord doesn't lose any money on me!

I'd give anything to go back to work. It's hard for me not to work. I go nuts. I'm so used to being active. And I was always around people. I miss that. I can't crochet anymore since my hand went on the bum. And sometimes I can't even embroider.

I understand what it's like for Grandma. She used to crochet all the time and now she can't anymore. It's hard for her; she's always done for herself and now she can't even get out of the house. She just looks at four walls and sleeps.

Around the time Mr. Nesbitt died, she started talking about dying. She even made a dress to be buried in—a white satin gown. But she doesn't talk about it anymore. When I was living over in Yakima I'd go see Grandma, and she'd be sitting with the TV pulled up close to her chair and the sound turned way up. I bet that didn't help her eyes. She could still read then, but in the last year Ruby has had to read her letters to her. Grandma can't see to do anything now.

Grandma's never been happy anywhere since she left that house where she was living when Tom Nesbitt died. It was just a two-room place; it wasn't even a house. All falling down, with only cold water and an outhouse. Grandma says she's never been happy out west here, but she's forgot. I know she was happy on the ranch at Roy. We used to pick wild strawberries and she'd make strawberry shortcake. They say when you get as old as her you return to your childhood. She calls Michigan her home now. But she wasn't happy when she was a child. She had nobody to play with. Her grandparents weren't affectionate. Just like her; she was never affectionate either. But of my kids, Bobby's always been Grandma's favorite. And she thinks the world of Bobby's kids because they'll sit and listen to her. That's all Grandma wants; someone to pay attention to her.

What would I do if I had everything to do over again? I guess I wouldn't have married so young. There are places I'd have liked to go that I haven't gone. You know, in the state of Washington you can see everything there is in the United States. We've got rain forests, sand dunes and deserts, mountains. I like the country over in Yakima best. In the spring when all the orchards are in bloom. And the hills are beautiful. They're never the same. They're green in the spring and again in the fall. Then the desert flowers bloom on them. It's real pretty.

Over here, in Tacoma, I don't have so many friends. I visit the neighbors sometimes, go to the mall in Tacoma. And I see Mom quite often now. Sometimes I spend the weekend with her. My sister Irene's here in town; I see her all the time. Annabel's in Olympia, so I don't see her too often. And Margaret, I see once a year. She's up about a hundred miles in the mountains. Irene's the only one of us that hasn't been married more than once. Annabel was married four times; Margaret, three times. I guess it must run in the family.

I guess Norm was the best of my marriages. The first time I got married I thought I was in love with him, and I guess I was. When I married Norm I thought I was in love with him. That lasted longer than any of them. The love with Norm lasted longer. He's dead. Buried in Yakima. I was sad when he died. I thought I was over him, but it kind of shook me up.

My kids Bill and Fran didn't have any divorces. Of course when I found out Bill was going to marry an older woman—she's close to my age—I didn't think that would work too well. But Jean's been good to that boy, and I like her. The main thing I objected to, older woman or not, was she already had five kids. And they had five more of their own. Bill has a stepson almost as old as Fran. But Jean takes good care of the kids, and Bill makes a good living, so I've got no complaints about the way they've managed.

Of course Bobby's had divorces. Bobby and me have always been more or less close. But I wasn't going to interfere when she was having trouble. I've never given any of my kids any advice. I let them work their own life out. I'm not going to be an interfering mother-in-law. I've always sympathized with Bobby, but I've told her: "I don't know what you should do. It's up to you. Whatever you want." Which I think is right. She's old enough to make up her own mind. Of course I could have told her that men never change. They say they will, but people don't change. That's the way they are and that's the way they're going to stay. Bobby'll make it all right. She's like I am. Independent.

I took a tranquilizer this morning. And one last night. I couldn't fall asleep. I listened to KGO from San Francisco most of the night. At midnight there's a talk show; then they play music and give the news. I fell asleep about five in the morning.

Barbara

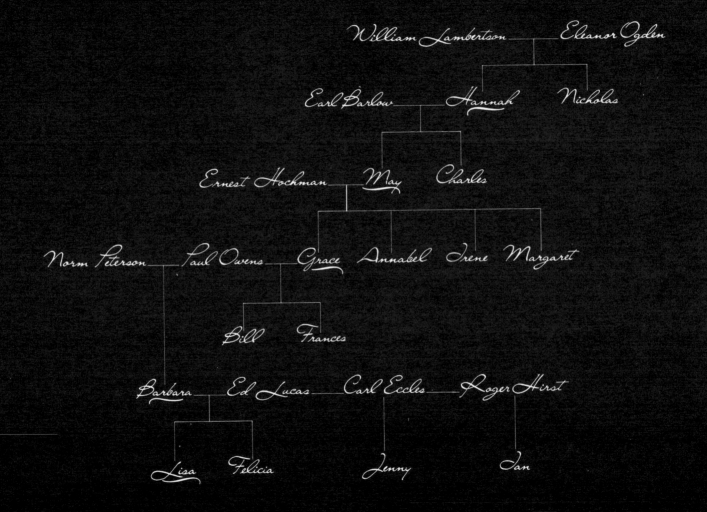

Barbara

Tacoma began life as a mill town in the last quarter of the nineteenth century. Other industries, and military installations, have grown up during the world wars, but day and night the stacks of the pulp mills, paper mills, lumber mills and smelters on the waterfront still stream tornadoes of smoke into the sky.

All Tacoma's energy seems concentrated on the waterfront. Above it, the city rises steeply for five or six blocks and then spreads out into a series of quiet, well-kept neighborhoods of small apartment buildings and one-family houses. Tacoma is a pleasant city: in the summer Wright Park is idyllic, with great shade trees making a light and dark mosaic of the rich green grass; blackberries and wild flowers grow on vacant lots; and on clear evenings there is the towering spectacle of Mount Rainier, salmon red in the setting sun.

But as with many American cities, Tacoma's center—even its newly built shopping mall—has too many vacant storefronts. By six o'clock in the evening, downtown is deserted. The small turn-of-the-century buildings on Commerce Street and Pacific Avenue cast shadows on streets as empty as an Edward Hopper painting. Farther down Pacific Avenue, a strip of bars with names like Diamond Duke's Tavern and the South Pacific Cafe offer go-go girls, pool and liquor to the servicemen from Fort Lewis and McCord Air Force Base. Apart from these and some other, more respectable bars and restaurants and three movie houses, there are few places to go in Tacoma. The old men who live on pensions at the Colonial Hotel sit in the lobby, their hats on, and read back issues of magazines. Most people seem to stay home and watch television.

Barbara was born in 1934; most of her life has been spent in Tacoma or Yakima. Her early childhood was in Yakima, the years of World War II in Tacoma, and she has moved back and forth as events have taken her.

With Barbara, I enter my own time in history: a childhood when the name of Franklin Roosevelt was synonymous with the word president; when, at dinnertime, all talk stopped and families listened intently to news of the London blitz or the Second Front; when, overnight it seemed, we were told that the Russians were no longer allies but enemies, and school children crouched under their desks waiting for the atom bomb to fall. And more than these momentous reference points, Barbara and I share a consciousness formed by the movies we saw, the radio serials we listened to, everything that colored the air of the 1940s and 50s.

When I met Barbara first in 1973, she was living in Tacoma with her third husband, the father of her fourth child. She had a granddaughter a little older than her son. When I saw her again, a year later, she was divorced, still living in the same house. Lisa, her oldest child, who was twenty-one, lived not far away with her own husband and child. The three younger children—Ian, two and a half, Jenny, eleven, and Felicia, seventeen, lived with Barbara. The burden of financial and emotional support for her family was then, as it had been most of her life, almost entirely Barbara's alone.

In a flat, unemphatic voice, Barbara talks about a life that is a caricature of what the lives of women of our generation were supposed to be—a fun-house mirror reflection, cruelly distorting the promises of love and marriage and family and "togetherness." Listening to her, I remember what May has said: "We got freedom in this country to do what we want to do." It is the common wisdom that persists even as we learn how that freedom is limited by the circumstances of our lives: how fear of poverty, loneliness, a sense of helplessness in controlling events dictate our choices and truncate our hopes as surely as a tyrant would. So that when we are trapped by the consequences of our "free" choice, the failure is personal and we are alone with it.

In its externals Barbara's life is not very different from Grace's, May's or Hannah's; the cycle is repeated. But for me, everything culminates with Barbara. The lives of the Lambertson women are no anomaly. Barbara's time is my time too, and if my own circumstances have been less desperate than hers, still I understand very well the direction of her impulses, the extent of her self-doubt, the inability to imagine options.

Fran & Barbara:
Yakima, 1937

Barbara: 1934-1952

It's funny the things you remember. I must have been two or three years old when we moved to Yakima. The house we lived in was way back on the lot, and it had a big hedge up next to the road. A big, tall hedge about six or seven feet tall, and we had a big yard to play in. My sister and brother and I used to pack peanut butter sandwiches and walk to a park quite a ways away. And this fellow my dad worked for, his parents lived on the way to the park, and we used to stop and have lunch in their yard and she'd always bring out Kool-Aid.

I must have been only about three or four when Dad had a car accident. I saw him pull his car out in the road and another car hit him broadside, demolished the car. Dad wasn't hurt, but I never forgot it.

And then Dad built a house. He built it by himself. It was a big, tall house and we moved into it when it was only half finished. We had acreage there; not too much, but we had a cow and a garden. And in the front there was an open irrigation ditch, and you had to go over a bridge to come in. To water the garden you just opened the gates of the ditch and let the water come in over the lawn and flood it.

We had a cow then that wouldn't stay in the pasture. She'd jump the fences all the time and we'd have to chase her down. She'd go across the street to the orchard and eat the apples and pears. We raised pigs then, and rabbits too. Everything we raised, we ate. The rabbits, chickens, everything. A couple of the rabbits we kept for pets, and they were the ones that had babies all the time. We used to let them out of their hutches, and they'd go over to the orchard and eat the fallen fruit and come in at night and sleep under their hutches. I remember, I used to like to watch Dad kill the big roosters. You know, when they cut their heads off and then let them go they throw blood all over. It's really terrible, really ugly, but to us it was funny. We never even thought about it. When you're raised like that, it doesn't bother you.

I always did everything with Dad. If he was hammering nails, I always had to be with him. If he was working on the car, I had to help him. And he was very gentlemanly; he'd let me. One time, before I started school, he killed a pig and hung it. Mr. Lovell was helping him, and they told me to go in the house and fix lunch for them because they didn't want me to watch. But I snuck out and watched anyway, and then I fixed lunch. I heard Dad talk about that lunch since; he said the coffee was absolutely like mud. I couldn't have been more than four and a half or five. That was funny, having such a little kid fix lunch, just to get me out of their hair so I wouldn't watch what they were doing.

I don't remember much about that house Dad built. Our kitchen was really big and we had a wood stove to cook on and we had to keep pails of water in front of it. We used to get baby chicks in the spring, and we'd keep them in cardboard cartons in the kitchen, where it was warm, because they were too little to go outside. When they got bigger, we ate them. That house never got completely finished because Dad got sick. He got sleeping sickness, from a horsefly bite, I think it was. Not too many people survive from it.

We had an outdoor bathroom in that house, and I remember Mom used to walk him back and forth from the bathroom and he didn't even know it. He was asleep all

Fran & Barbara: Yakima, 1938

Barbara: 1939

Barbara: 1940

the time. Finally they brought an ambulance to take him to the hospital. It backed up to the front door and got stuck. The town only had one ambulance, so they had to send a hearse out to take him to the railroad station so they could get him to the hospital in Tacoma. Dad had to ride in the baggage car because he had to stay on the stretcher; Mom went with him in the boxcar, and the neighbor lady, Mrs. Johnson, stayed with us on the train until we got over here and went to my aunt's. I don't think I really understood what was going on. Everything seemed so strange. He was in the hospital for three or four months, and they didn't think he was going to live. But then he was over it and we went back to Yakima.

When we went back they sold that house Dad was building, and we moved into another little house right by school, just outside the town. That was a dinky little house; it only had two bedrooms. But it was a lot of fun being right across the street from school, because we could always play on the slides and swings on the school grounds.

From there we moved closer to town. And every Sunday before we went to Sunday school, we got our dime. After Sunday school we'd all get to go to the show. We saw Roy Rogers and Hopalong Cassidy. And they used to have these funny little serials where every Sunday you'd just see a piece of it, and you'd have to come next Sunday 'cause you don't want to miss it. Where women would fall off cliffs, and things like that.

And then, later on, they started vaudeville in the theater downtown, and every Saturday they'd have two vaudeville shows. It was mostly amateur talent things. I think they were affiliated with Major Bowes. My cousin, Dad's niece, came clear over

Barbara:
1934-1952

197

from Tacoma once to be in it, and to us it was a big thrill to see our cousin up there tap-dancing. It was fun. Bill, Fran, me, all the kids in the neighborhood went.

When I was little, Yakima was really funny. The Front Street area, where you cross the railroad tracks—that was full of migrant workers, bums, people like that. On the right-hand side was the Alaskan Corral, and the movie theater we went to used to be on the left-hand side. It was a big treat for us to walk down there. Yakima Avenue was a brick street then, real narrow, nothing like it is now. The town stopped right at the railroad tracks; the whole town was only four or five blocks long. There was a J.C. Penney, I remember; it was an old-fashioned kind of store with big bow glass windows. My uncle Charlie used to sit out in front of it. He made wooden names and things like that, and they let him put up a card table in front of the store and sell his things there. The store used to have wooden floors, oily, really old, and they'd squeak when you walked on them. They didn't have cash registers; the woman up on the balcony had the money, and the clerks would put their money in little tubes and put them on a line and pull a handle, and the tubes shot up to her and she'd send change down in them. Oh, that used to fascinate us.

The curbs on the sidewalks weren't very high; one time it rained real hard and the water went over the curbs and flooded all the stores' basements.

We used to go to the depot a lot too. The depot used to be a real center. People just would come there and hang around and talk. There were always trains coming and going, and there was a little restaurant across the street. Now, of course, all the depots are dead.

The big Chinook Hotel that's there now, that was just a skeleton for years. They

Norm Peterson &
Walter McCo
1940

Barbara & her father. 1943

Barbara: 1946

used to call it the Skeleton Building. I imagine it was probably during the Depression that they stopped building it. I didn't notice the Depression at all. When I think back, the only way I can remember anything is that we raised everything we ate ourselves. And the first Christmas I really remember, our Christmas present was that Mom made doll clothes for these big twin dolls my sister and I had. She made them out of scraps from the clothes she made us. And we didn't have too many clothes either. I had maybe two dirndl skirts and a couple of blouses. And you didn't throw anything away. Everything was used.

It was a lot of fun in Yakima when I was a kid. We used to go fishing sometimes, take a picnic lunch and spend the day fishing. In half an hour you're up in the hills and you can be all alone in the woods. When we'd go to Tacoma to visit the grandmas, maybe three times a year, we had a car with a rumble seat, and in the winter and in early spring we'd have to put blankets over us because it was so cold. It used to take five or six hours to come across the mountains. The cars couldn't take the hills and we'd have to stop and get water to cool them off. My uncle Charlie had a camper that, when you opened it up, looked like a teepee. Inside it had two full-size beds on both sides. And every summer we used to go up in the mountains, really high up. The cars would have to ford the creeks to get up where we always went. It was a wilderness then, just a dirt road to it. Years later we drove up there and it's blacktop road all the way; you can get up there in twenty minutes.

And then there were county fairs once a year. They were like small carnivals —rides, that type of thing. You'd see all the kids you knew—the 4-H kids showing their animals and what they'd grown. And they had Grange Halls too, you know, and everybody came in for spaghetti feeds and dinners. That was a big thing. They'd have them once a month, I think. The Grange members, the women, made the food. I'd go with the neighbor kids; my folks didn't go too much. I guess because it was mainly for farmers, to give farmers a chance to get together and discuss their crops. I remember the older people talking about how they used to have quilting bees.

I started school in Yakima when I was five. My mother got special permission from the school board to let me start early. For my first report card, all I got was a note because I wasn't of age. It said that next time I would get a real report card, but that I was doing real well. I liked school. It was a country school and that's a different thing. I don't know how to explain it. There's no class distinction. No cliques, no clannish groups. I guess because most people in the country are more of a poorer class. Well, I don't really mean it that way, but they don't care as much about their clothes— everybody lives on the same level. And everybody goes to all the things. Like you have ball games after school and everybody plays. It didn't matter if you were in the third grade or fifth grade, they'd let you play. The families, most of them, have been there for years and everybody knows everybody else. I knew most of the kids from the Grange Hall before I even got to school.

I learned to read in school. The teacher who taught me to really enjoy books was Mrs. Norton, my third- and fourth-grade teacher. She was really strict, but I got along with her because I was always a good student. I liked work. And when she found out I was interested in books, she'd give me books to read and, after, we'd talk about the stories. She made me understand that there's really a story behind it, and really understand it. I read some Dickens and Mark Twain. Some of those were too deep for me, and I'd have to put them away and then go back to them.

I was always reading books. I read *Heidi* three or four times when I was a kid. And *The Secret Garden,* about this little girl who's hired to be a companion to this little crippled boy whose mother is dead. There was a nurse, and the dad was gone all the time. It was real mysterious. And the little girl found a key to get into this secret garden where the father would never let anyone go in, because that's where the mother had died and the boy had got crippled. She started taking the boy in there and he started walking. That was a beautiful story.

I read a couple of the *Little Women* books, but they didn't interest me. I read fairy tales when I was littler. Grandma had a big book of Grimms. And the Lassie series. I loved them. I loved animal stories. You kind of live in a fantasy world when you're reading them.

I think I read every book in the library. I loved Daphne du Maurier and books about Victorian days when there were still pirates. *The Black Hawk* was one of my favorites; it was about a young man who was a pirate in a way, but in another way he wasn't. I liked adventure stories. And stories about young girls who'd made a go of it. They'd go and work and do things. Mom got a book from a book club about a woman who had gotten into politics and became a very strong person. But she didn't really want to be a politician or the head of a big corporation. She wanted to be a woman.

Mom would get so mad at me. "Put down that book and get out here and do the dishes!" If I didn't have work to do she didn't mind me reading, but invariably I got

Barbara, her last picture with long hair: 1947

into a corner and was reading when I was supposed to be doing something else. I used to get spankings for arguing over the dishes and not doing what I was told. We kids had chores to do—dust, help with the wash, wring it out, help iron. And we always had to do the dishes. I can't remember Dad ever spanking me. I always knew when he said something I'd better do it, but I wasn't scared of him. I was always helping him do things.

Mom was always very strict, and Dad was easy-going. You didn't get out of hand with him, but he was easier-going. Mom picked a lot. She picked and yelled about everything. I can remember her picking and yelling at Dad like she did with us kids. Later, when she went to work, we were supposed to keep the house clean. And at that time my brother and I had a big paper route. I'd be out doing the route, and then she'd yell because I didn't have the housework done. It's hard to remember what I thought then, but Mom, I think, always wanted something. I don't know what it was, but she never had it.

Besides books, I used to love the radio. What I remember mostly is we always used to sit around it on Sunday afternoons and listen to the serials. "First-Nighter," "Mystery Theatre," "The Shadow." We sat glued to the radio and sometimes we did our school work in front of it. There was one radio in the living room, one of those consoles, and we used to sit on the floor with our ears right up to the speaker. "First-Nighter" was my favorite show. Mr. First-Nighter would welcome you to the theater and introduce the play. He had such a beautiful voice. Years later I saw him on TV and I couldn't believe it. He was a balding, short little man. And "Captain Midnight." I hated Ovaltine, but you had to drink it to get decoder rings and things.

I made Mom buy it so I could get the seals to decode those messages he gave at the end.

I was six when they bombed Pearl Harbor. I vaguely remember it. We all listened to the six o'clock news every day. I guess it was with Gabriel Heatter. He had that funny little voice that never changed. And there was someone else who'd say, "There's good news *tonight.*"

I don't remember any war news from then. I knew there was a war, but it was far away. The only thing that brought it home was my cousin being killed. He was my dad's nephew, Jimmy Hullett. He went into the Marine Corps, and he had been in the Philippines. He came home on leave and came over to see us. I must have been in the third grade, and he came to school one day in his uniform and talked to my class about the Philippines and the natives. And I was so proud! I'll never forget that. I was walking about *that* far above everyone else.

He'd just gotten married on his leave. He had the prettiest wife! She had long red hair, and she'd let me sit and comb it and brush it for hours. And he and his brothers would always hold me and play with me and show a lot of love and affection.

The day before Jimmy had to leave, everybody went downtown and had a few drinks and then they started walking right up the middle of Yakima Avenue. Jimmy was half-shot, and the police came and escorted him because he was in his full dress Marine uniform; they gave him an escort in those three-wheel motorcycles they had at the time. You didn't see many service people in Yakima. It was a big thrill to have him there.

207

He'd been a paratrooper and he had a lot of medals. He transfered to the ground troops because he was afraid that if he went back as a paratrooper he'd never come home. And then he went back and was killed. The first place he was sent, he was killed. Iwo Jima. That was really a shock. Especially after spending those few days with us. It just broke my heart. Mom and Dad told me about it, and Dad cried and cried. Jimmy was his favorite nephew. It made us understand what war was really like. Before that, it wasn't such a big thing.

I was in the fifth grade when we moved over to Tacoma. I was real sad about leaving Yakima. We had a horse at the time, and I didn't want to leave it, or the neighborhood. There were a lot of kids all the same age, and everybody did things as a group; we all played together. It didn't matter that I was the littlest kid, I always got to play anyway. Dad had a pickup truck, and everytime he'd leave to go someplace, all the kids in the neighborhood would get in the back of the pickup. It was just a nice, fun neighborhood, real friendly. We were a little excited about moving, because we'd be with all the grandmas and the relatives. But leaving the horse and the friends and the life, it was real hard.

I hadn't seen the grandmas much when we lived in Yakima. Maybe three times a year we'd go over there. Little Grandma—that's what we called Grandma Nesbitt—lived in a small place in Algona, I remember. She was married to Tom Nesbitt; we kids didn't know about her other husbands. Her dad lived with her. And her dad's brother. No, that was *her* brother, Nick. I couldn't keep them straight. You know, when you're a kid all old people look the same age. Grandma McCormack lived on Steilacoom Lake, outside Tacoma, and when we'd go over we'd stay with her. They had a couple of cabins on their property, and we'd stay in one of them.

It was a different story over here in Tacoma from Yakima. It was a shock, really. We lived in the project they built for people working in the war. The school was just a wooden building thrown together. They put us on split shifts because our school got too crowded; everyone was coming over to work in the shipyards. Mom was going out of her mind because the house was full of kids half the time.

A lot of the kids were from big towns, and I wasn't used to them. It really kind of scared me. That's when I became a straight-A student. I just did my work and tried to please the teacher. But I remember we used to play marbles a lot and the kids would get mad at me because I was such a tomboy.

It was such a tense time over here, so close to McCord Air Force Base and Fort Lewis. Everybody was so afraid something was going to happen. We never had air raid drills in school in Yakima, but we did when we came over to Tacoma. There was a big canyon in back of the project, and we kids decided we'd go down there to live if anything happened. We used to play there, and we had all these trails that would be our hiding places if they ever bombed us.

At school they had it worked out that if we were bombed, the buses would take us on the road toward Mount Rainier, west. But Mom worked on Center Street, and she would have gone the other way. And Dad, when he was working at the mill in Auburn, he would have gone the opposite way. That used to worry us. How would we ever get back together if something happened? Everybody would be separated.

Barbara:
1934-1952

209

I remember when the war started they picked up the Japanese farmers and put them in concentration camps. My dad's sister had a fruit and vegetable stand in Auburn, and she'd always buy fruits and vegetables from the Japanese farmers. Then they picked them up and put them in a compound with barbed wire and little barracks-type buildings. All their land just went to nothing. They had the most beautiful farms. I've never seen anything like them since the war. The lettuce, it would be in straight rows, no matter which angle you looked at it from. Not a weed in it. Just like a postcard. Just beautiful. And then, six months later, all their fields were weeds.

I remember some of the grown-ups saying, "Well, some of them might be spies." There was talk then that the Japanese had planned to bomb Seattle and Bremerton but the planes didn't get through. And the grown-ups said that some of the Japanese farmers must be spies who told them where the shipyards were. I thought it was funny that these average little farmers could be spies. But then you'd see war movies about how farmers *were* spies, and I got to thinking that maybe they were.

My mother started working a while after we moved over here. At the laundry, where my grandma and aunt worked. I knew they were having problems, my dad and her. I knew because he left us a couple of times. He went to live with his mother in Auburn. At the time I was taking guitar lessons, and he used to come in and get me and take me to my lesson every Thursday. He didn't stay away too long; of course it seemed like years to me, but it was just a matter of a week or two. Then he was just back. Nobody explained anything to us.

I think they had two split-ups in Tacoma. In Yakima they seemed to be getting along fine. I didn't notice anything. It's hard for a kid to realize what your parents' problem is. I thought it was just moving over to Tacoma. I think if we hadn't moved, they'd never have had any problems. Over here, it was just the quicker pace of life, being with the rest of the relatives and pulling between the two sets of in-laws. There was a lot of bickering: "Let's go to see *my* mother this Sunday." "No, we'd better go see *my* mother." "We always go to your mother's; why can't we go to my mother's?" That type thing. And when us kids would go to visit the relatives, they'd start arguing then over where we were going to stay. Actually, I guess there were a lot of problems. When we moved over to Tacoma we were just always too busy to have fun. The hills are too far to go to; we went a few times, but it just wasn't the same. There was a different feeling in the family.

Except for those two times Dad left, I didn't pay too much attention to what was going on at home. I was going to school and doing homework. And going to movies. All those big, musical extravaganzas with those big pyramids, and all those beautiful dresses. And Esther Williams movies. I really liked those. I didn't like movies that had stories so much, because you end up crying. I loved the Lassie movies and *Bambi*. You usually cry in those too, but it's a different kind of emotion.

Fran and I always used to buy the hit parade magazines. We had all the words to the songs so we could sing along with the radio. We'd play the folks' record player at full blast, and of course they'd come home and we'd have to turn it down. In those days it was Bing Crosby and the Ames Brothers and the Andrews Sisters. Frank Sinatra was just starting, and I remember my dad used to think it was terrible the way all the girls acted over him.

In school we had square dancing. When I was in the sixth grade, the straight-A students got to go to the junior high school; they'd teach us to square dance there, and we'd come back and teach the rest of the kids. My sister tried to teach me the Avalon, but I was never much of a dancer. I was too much of a tomboy; she used to get so mad at me. Sometimes she'd take me to dances at the Y on Saturday nights.

My sister and I shared a room—we always slept together—and it was just plastered with movie star pictures. On my side I had Doris Day and Frank Sinatra, Judy Garland. I liked Clark Gable and Errol Flynn, but mostly I liked women. I loved Susan Hayward especially. The one role I remember most of hers was when she played an Army nurse and got buried in a bombing. It took them days to find her and she was in shock; it took her months to come out of it. She was kind of tragic. Doris Day was the opposite, a kind of happy-go-lucky teen-ager type. I used to buy *Photoplay* and *Modern Screen* to read about them. In those days there wasn't as much garbage in the movie magazines. Just about their pasts and their families.

I remember when the war ended. We heard it on the radio. Downtown Tacoma was just packed with people. You couldn't move, and everybody was kissing everybody. It was really something. That was V-E Day. It was absolutely wild. I didn't think there *were* that many people. At first it just didn't seem possible that it was really over. We all went downtown for a while and then came home. For days the papers were full of big pictures of the mobs in New York and here celebrating.

Then they dropped the A-bomb, and I remember the pictures of how the people were burned and the millions who died. Pictures of the city before and then after the bomb. After, there was just nothing. We knew something about the A-bomb because there was an atomic center about a hundred miles outside Yakima, in Hanford. There were a lot of people who worked there and lived in Yakima because there wasn't enough housing. All we knew was that it was some big, scary thing you had to be afraid of, because they had to bury things in the ground with cement all around them. Everybody who worked there had to wear badges with their pictures on it. It was all very secretive.

When Roosevelt died I remember there was a big thick special edition of the newspaper. And people were crying. I think I cried because everybody else did. But you know, in those days things didn't seem so close to you. We'd see things in newsreels, but that was maybe a week after they happened.

After Roosevelt was dead and the war was all over, I can remember people saying that FDR gave the Russians Manchuria and now they were taking everything. Everybody blamed him for giving in to the Russians; they were saying we shouldn't have stopped where we did, we should have gone right through Russia. It was confusing, because I thought we were allies and I remember how happy everybody was when the Russian and American soldiers met in Berlin. That Communist thing got to be really something. Everyone was afraid their best friend was a card-carrying Communist. People were saying some of the unions were Communistic, and you'd hear about Alger Hiss and all that spy stuff. And McCarthy was investigating everything he could get his hands on. It seemed so elaborate. But it could be true. You never know what's going on.

I don't exactly remember when we moved back to Yakima. It was after the war. Dad had been working on the railroad in Tacoma, and then he had quit that and gone to work in a sawmill. I thought we were going to move up to North Bend, where the mill operator bought a new mill. We had gone up and looked at a little house there. Then, all of a sudden, we just drove back home to Yakima. I don't know when Mom and Dad decided to go back. But you know how you do, when you're trying to straighten things out; you think if you go back to where everything was all right, maybe things will be better.

I was in the eighth grade when we went back. All my close friends lived on the opposite side of town, so I didn't really see them again till I got to high school. But we didn't really become friends again. Except for Doreen, who's still a friend. I was a junior in high school when Mom left. She just walked out and left us.

I didn't know what was happening at home. I knew Mom and Dad fought about money. He'd always give her his paychecks, sign them over to her. She handled all the money. They'd quarrel about little things, like not having enough money to go someplace or buy something for the house. But it didn't seem like very much.

I was the only one at home when Mom left. Fran was baby-sitting, living with this family in the country. And Billy was in the Navy. Billy used to run away from home all the time. He was forever running away. Sometimes he'd come back himself; sometimes Dad would find him. The last time he ran away I think he got tangled up with the police and they brought him back. That's when he joined the Navy. He was seventeen then. He was a good kid, a funny kid. I don't know what his problem was; we weren't that close. I don't know why he kept running away—whether Mom was too strict, or maybe, her way of going about being strict.

Mom and I were never that close when I was little. She wasn't ever very loving, never kissing us good night or things like that. But I wasn't so old that I didn't need her. And she just left. It really hurt.

My dad was really broken up, too. He was really in bad shape. I was going with a kid named Carl Eccles then, and we got permission to take his folks' car and we drove over to Auburn and brought my dad's mother back with us. It helped Dad a lot, calmed him down. Mom was staying with Little Grandma until she got her own apartment, and my auntie and I went over there and talked to her, begged her to come back. But she wouldn't. I don't know, I guess she just had to get away.

Dad didn't want to stay in the house we were living in then. We sold everything. I'll never forget it, because we had had all that furniture since I was a little teeny kid. The davenport was one of those real dark-blue ones, with material that looks like velvet, except thicker, and it had a curved back and big curved arms. We had an old-fashioned buffet, real dark wood, with a mirror over it. Oh, and a rocking chair—Grandaddy's rocker, Little Grandma's father. It looked like bamboo and it had rawhide interwoven for the seat and back. We lost a lot of things like that. My dad wanted to get rid of all the memories.

Barbara: 1948

Barbara: 1949

Fran went back east after Mom left. To Ohio. To her real dad. One of Mom's sisters helped her and Bill find him. They contacted the Navy department and found out that he had turned himself in for desertion after years and years. You know, it's funny. All the years when we were kids, Fran and Billy worshipped my dad. But they always felt that *I* was his child and they weren't. They felt he treated me differently. It wasn't true, but they felt it. And then when Mom left and we sold the furniture and moved to an apartment, Fran would never ask Dad for money for school or anything. She'd always ask me to ask him. It wasn't that she didn't love him or he didn't love her. She just felt, I think, that she didn't belong. And her mother had deserted, so what did she have left? So when she found her real dad, she went back there. I don't know how long she stayed, not too long, though. And my brother went back, too. I can't remember if they went back together or if Fran went first and Bill went when he was on leave. Their father was married and he had children, eight children, I think. But he had never divorced my mother. My mother had never divorced him either; she and my dad didn't get married until he'd been declared dead, after seven years. So Mom was free to marry then but he wasn't. Anyway—this is just what I heard; I never talked to my sister about it: sometime after Fran and Bill got to Ohio, their Dad took off, left his wife and kids. When Bill got out of the Navy he went back there, to Ohio, and he brought his dad's wife out to Yakima, her and her children. He's married to her now. I think they have six children of their own. I don't know how my mother felt about the wedding. I never talked to her about it.

I never knew that my mom and dad weren't married when I was born. I found that out after she left. When she left she didn't think to take her trunk, and I found my birth certificate in there and all the marriage licenses. That was really shattering. Because on my birth certificate my dad wasn't even listed as my dad. Mom put her first husband down as my father. So legally, I wasn't my dad's child. My dad didn't even know that. He knew they weren't married, but he didn't think she would go that far—not even to put him down as the father! I showed it to him and he just cried. It was bad enough having her leave, but that really shattered him. Him and me both. I don't think Mom even knows I know that. No, she must know, because she knew that Dad had my name legally changed in court. But we never talked about it.

After we sold everything, Dad and me moved into a basement apartment across the street from a tavern. Mom had got an apartment downtown. One time, I remember, Dad went down there and broke her door in. She had a boyfriend there, a fellow she worked with. And then Dad started running around too. He started going out with a waitress. I liked Nancy, but then he started bringing her home nights, and in those days that was really a taboo thing. I was just sixteen at the time. My dad was always my idol. We were real close, and it hurt me more than anything, I think. Lots of times he'd leave home on Friday nights and come back in time to be at work Monday mornings. I'd be alone in that apartment all weekend.

I didn't know what to do. Once I went over to see Grandma McCormack to ask if she'd help, try to talk to Mom. But she didn't know what to say to her. I don't think she knew that Mom didn't take me with her. Grandma McCormack was always very good to us kids, but I hadn't been around her much, so I was probably a little afraid of

Barbara, 9th grade graduation: 1949

her. And you can tell, with her, if you're talking about something she doesn't want to talk about. She closes off on very personal things. She's probably not sure of herself. And I didn't go to Little Grandma, because Mom had been there and Little Grandma knew. I used to go and visit her, but we never talked about it. I probably knew it was something nobody wanted to talk about.

I had started going with Carl about six months before the folks split up; his grandparents were super people. I was so unhappy being alone in that apartment, feeling I'd lost touch with everything and everybody. And there wasn't anybody to help me and they said I could come live with them. And his parents were really good to me, too. They were everything I wanted my parents to be like. Just very happy. They didn't quarrel. I never once saw them quarrel. His mother didn't work. She was always home, and dinner was always ready and lunch was always set. It represented something to me that I'd always wanted. I don't know how to say it—like nothing was a very big chore to her. Everything she did had a purpose. Nothing looked out of place, and yet there'd be lots of company, people all over the house. *My* mother would get very nervous when we had company. Things just never went smooth at home. And with Carl's mother, everything always went smoothly. She was one of those kinds of people who can handle everything and never get flustered. The atmosphere was quiet; there were never any kinds of pressure.

And his grandfather Calvin was just like a grandpa to me. I lived with him and his wife on their fruit ranch. They grew apples and pears and peaches, a few apricots; and Calvin couldn't lift the apple boxes to stack them on the truck. They were very heavy, forty, fifty pounds. I'd lift them and stack them for him, and he used to make me feel so proud that I could help him like that.

I stayed with them all summer. And I remember that his wife got me material to make my school clothes for the fall. The sewing machine was upstairs in the attic and I'd go up there and sew. It was so hot up there. But they bought me all the material. After I left them I used to go back to visit, and I always got a big hug and tears would come into their eyes. They just really cared, and it made me feel so good that I meant something to them. They treated me just like a daughter.

I was going into my senior year of high school then, and I was so shy I could hardly talk to people. I couldn't stand up in front of the class and give an oral report. I've have it all prepared and then when I'd get called on I'd say I wasn't prepared. I got all A's except in that kind of work. I remember in the senior year you had to go behind the podium and give a fifteen-minute speech. My speech was going to be about Russian Communism. I did a lot of reading for it and I had it all prepared. I was going to say that Communism is really an ideal situation but that it's almost an impossible thing to make work—that people aren't made that way unless they're raised that way. You can't take free people and put them in that sort of environment and expect them to be happy. I really worked hard on that speech, and when I went to give it I was so scared I didn't breathe. I just kept talking and passed out. That's how shy I was. That's how bad it was for me then. I had one group of friends and that was it. I couldn't even really talk to other kids.

I had started going with Carl when I was a sophomore. He was my first love, I guess you'd call it. It was the first time I had sex and it meant something, it really did. Then, after the folks split up, he was all I had. I didn't really think about it that way at the time, but I guess it was something stable in my life.

I don't know why we broke up. I think it was . . . I wanted to go back to my dad and I didn't know how. I felt trapped where I was. His folks were so good to me, but I felt like if I stayed with them I'd never get back to my dad or my mother again. I was getting too far away from them, and it scared me. I really didn't know what I was doing; it's so hard to think why you do what you do when you're a kid, but we broke up and Carl went into the service. After that, I couldn't stay out at the ranch. I felt awkward. I was just floating around. I didn't belong anyplace. I didn't know what to do. I didn't have any money or anything.

I went to Mom's and asked if I could live with her. She said she couldn't afford to keep me to finish high school. So I went to the school counselor, and he sent me to live with this little old lady who wanted someone to stay with her at night. She lived in an old kind of hotel-type building. There was a big room where all the old people sat and watched TV. And they had little teeny bedrooms. She had a cot in hers that I was supposed to sleep on. I'll never forget that. All night long I lay there and watched the neon lights on Yakima Avenue going on and off and off and on. I couldn't live like that.

If Dad would have given me fifty dollars a month I could have lived at the Y. But I was afraid to go ask him. I was afraid he was mad at me for leaving. I decided what I'd do was go down to the railroad yards where he worked and get some money from

Barbara, high school graduation: 1951

him so I could go over to Tacoma to my aunt's. I thought maybe she'd keep me. A bunch of kids came with me to the yards because there were a lot of bums down there. The bums used to live in little grass huts, and there'd been some murders. When we got there I found out that Dad didn't even work there anymore. They'd transferred him to the lower valley. He wasn't in Yakima at all.

Well, I found out where Dad was living. My grandpa had bought a house, and Dad was living in it and fixing it up for him. Grandpa always did that: bought houses and fixed them up and sold them. I asked Dad if I could stay with him. He said okay. He wasn't mad at me; we just didn't talk about anything that had happened. Dad and I lived together, but it was a you-go-your-way—I'll-go-my-way type of situation. He was still trying so hard to get over Mom. He was trying so hard, and drinking a lot at the time. He just kind of lost track of everything.

That house we lived in was all the way out on the other side of town. There was just one bus in the morning and one in the afternoon. If I missed the school bus, I had to walk five miles to school. I was working nights at the dime store, and Dad used to come in and get me. We had no phone, no nothing. We didn't have any furniture either. The bed I had, I think it was a studio couch. And I used to heat water on the wood stove to wash Dad's clothes by hand. The place was all tore up; we were just living in the kitchen and one other room.

I didn't know any of the neighbors or anything and I got real sick one weekend. I had the flu so bad I couldn't get my head off the pillow. We didn't have an inside bathroom. I was just really sick and having to go in and out to the outhouse. Dad was in Seattle with a girl friend. He'd left right after work on Friday and didn't know I was

Barbara:
1934–1952

225

sick. But I felt really bad, hurt that he'd left me. The group of kids I was running around with, Susan and Amy and Dick and Smitty, we all sort of took care of each other. They'd always make sure I had a ride home if I missed the last bus and Dad didn't show up. And that weekend we were all supposed to go to a football game. The kids came out to get me, and Smitty told his folks how sick I was and they brought me into town. They left a note for Dad. He got really upset about that. I think it embarrassed him.

Christmas that year was really terrible. I bought a little Christmas tree and got some decorations from Grandpa and hung them. And I got some little presents at the dime store for Dad. I sat there all night waiting for him and he never came home. I had an apple box sitting in front of the window to put the tree on, and I had rushed home so I could get the tree ready for when he got home. It was just a little tree, because I didn't have much money. He never showed up. God, I'll never forget that. I sat there and cried all night.

I graduated high school in January. There wasn't a real graduation ceremony, because it was midterm and there were only about five of us graduating at that time. We were going around the halls telling everybody good-bye and waiting in the halls between classes, and the teachers kicked us out. Isn't that terrible?

The school had gotten me this afternoon job during my last month in school, and then, when I graduated, I had it full time. It was a bookkeeping job at an auto parts place. I'd taken the business course in high school, so I knew how to keep books and take shorthand and stuff. When I started work full time I moved into town. My girl friend Elsa and I got an apartment together. It was in the same building where my mother lived, so I saw her a lot then. I don't think her life was going too well. She was partying a lot. I think she probably started drinking then. You know, even when I was in high school I can remember the three of us—Mom, Fran and me—going into town, and everybody thought we were sisters. Mom looked just like we did. But in a matter of a few years she just got really down. I don't know; drinking can be the ruination of a person.

Just a little bit after I moved into Mom's building she started going with a fellow she married. He was about ten years younger than her. It didn't last very long. Mom didn't like to talk about it, but I think he got picked up for indecent exposure or something like that. I don't know what it was about Mom. It was like she always had a dream. I don't know what the dream was. I don't think she knew what it was. But she never, ever could find it.

Barbara:
1934-1952

Barbara: 1952-1960

In the spring of 1952 I decided I'd better leave Yakima. Mom had left by that time to go to work in Bremerton. And Fran was married and living in Tacoma. Elsa, my girl friend, had moved out of the apartment, so I was living alone. One day I went swimming and my legs cramped really bad, and the doctor thought I had rheumatic fever or something. He said I'd have to quit work. And there I was all alone. And what are you going to do?

It wasn't rheumatic fever; it was a calcium deficiency. I hadn't been eating right, I guess—I'd have maybe a bowl of soup or something like that for dinner—and they gave me pills and shots for it. But when they told me I couldn't work, that scared me. If you can't work, you can't eat. That really scared me. If I were over in Tacoma I'd at least have Fran or Grandma McCormack if something happened. My girl friends in Yakima would take care of me if they knew I was sick, but it's not the same as having a relative. And I don't like to ask for help. That's a family trait. The whole family is like that.

I had started going out with Ed Lucas that June before I was going to leave Yakima. He was quiet, thoughtful, wanting to please all the time. Anything I wanted, he'd do. He wasn't pushy about anything. And he was a very handsome man; about six feet tall, funny, crooked nose, high cheekbones. I'd gone to school with his brother but I didn't meet him until Jim, Fran's husband, introduced us. Ed was about five or six years older than I was. He'd just gotten out of the Navy at that time. We got married in August.

I don't think we actually talked about it. Ed knew I was leaving Yakima, and, when I was going over to Tacoma, Hal Gurney and his wife drove us so I wouldn't have to take the bus. On the way they said, "Well, why don't you guys just get married?" And then Ed said that I shouldn't look for a job in Tacoma, because he was going to work up in the woods and we'd live up there. So I never actually got to say yes or no.

When you're younger you think of love as seeing someone across the room and your eyes meet and it's like lightning. That's the magic idea of it. I guess it was my idea of it. This was so quick, with Ed. Everything was going so fast I didn't have time to think about it. Now, I think I needed the security; that's really what it offered me.

I told Mom and Grandma when we got over here. They were happy about it, but they wanted us to wait a little until I could invite more of the relatives. But we didn't want to wait. My mother had to go to court with us to get the license because I wasn't eighteen, and we asked them to waive the three-day waiting period because Ed had to get up to the mountains to go to work.

So we just went to the Assembly of God church in Tacoma, on August fifteenth. My sister and her husband and Mom and Grandma McCormack were at the wedding. I remember I wore a pale-green faille tailored suit and a white hat, just a little band with net on it. And I had a white bag and gloves and pumps with little heels. It was early on a Friday afternoon and no one was in the church but us. Afterwards, we went to Grandma's and cut the cake and had cake and coffee and opened the few gifts we got.

Little Grandma didn't come to the wedding; it was too short notice for her to come all the way from Yakima; she sent us a crocheted tablecloth with a pineapple design. We got some towels and linens. I think I got sheets from Mom and towels from Grandma McCormack. Then Fran and Jim and Ed and me went to a Chinese restaurant. It was funny, because Ed didn't know how to drive; I knew how, but I didn't have a license yet and we didn't have a car. So Fran and Jim had to take us to the motel and pick us up the next morning. It was really comical. I was feeling really happy and all, really good then. The next day all four of us went to Woodland Park in Seattle, and we spent the day together and stayed at the Olympic Hotel in Seattle that night. Then, on Monday, we went up to Morton. It's a little logging town in the mountains. We moved in with Ed's sister and her husband.

It was a small house, only two bedrooms, really cramped. And they had a new baby, so you can imagine. The house was about ten miles out of town. The only way to get into town, if you didn't have a car, was to ride with the mailman. It was funny. The mailman sold bread, too.

The men would get up at dawn. Trucks would pick them up; it was a two-hour ride to get to where they were working. They'd leave at daylight and get back at dark. When it was raining, it was really bad; they'd come back just covered with mud. Ed was a choker—the one who puts the chain around the logs.

I helped Ed's sister with the baby and cleaned the house, and we'd sit around and talk and drink coffee. The well went dry that summer, and we had to go down to the river and throw a bucket on a rope off the bridge to get water. We did a lot of fishing. I used to go down to the river by myself a lot. There was a family of racoons there, and I'd sit and watch them, pick berries and walk around. When the men came home they were too tired to do anything. We ate dinner and talked, and then it was time for bed because they had to get up at three or four in the morning. I'd get up and make breakfast for them and then go back to bed. I liked being out in the country like that, but I didn't like living with other people. We were going to get a house of our own, but Ed decided he didn't like logging that much.

In November I came down to Tacoma to stay with my sister when her first baby was born. Fran and Jim lived next door to Grandma McCormack, and Grandma, Mom and I went through the whole labor with Fran. She had the baby at home.

The doctor came out to the house when her labor began, but he sat in the other room reading a book. Every once in a while he'd come in to see how things were going. When Fran's pains came, Mom or Grandma would get on one side of her and me on the other side, and we'd hold her hands. She'd put her knees against us and strain. I remember it was election night, the night Eisenhower was elected. We had the radio on because Fran and her husband were great Republicans and wanted him to win.

Fran was in such pain. She was crying and saying, "I'm *never* going to have another baby!" Now she has five. She didn't have any anesthetic except toward the end, when the doctor put her on his portable delivery table. The windows were wide open and the wind was whistling through, and Grandma kept saying Fran would catch cold. And the doctor said that a woman in labor can't catch anything. Grandma didn't want me to stay and watch the delivery—said I was too young. But she finally went home, and Mom and I took turns wiping Fran's brow. When she finally started to deliver, Jim was at her head, and the doctor told him how to give her ether—just a couple of drops, I remember. And Fran kept crying, "Jim, I don't want any more babies."

Then the doctor started working with her. He stretched her with his fingers so he wouldn't have to cut in the last stages. He had rubber gloves on and just really stretched her way out. Then he said, "Oh, here's the baby!" And I looked. I thought, "They've got to be kidding!" The head, when it goes through the pelvis, is all crushed, and the skin was all wrinkled up and it was kind of blue. It looked just like chicken intestines. And then as soon as the pressure of the pelvis was off, her little head just popped out. And the doctor said, "Uh oh, the cord's round her neck." And he held her and took the cord and slowly pulled it, slipped it from around her neck and then popped one shoulder and then the other. And there she was. She wasn't red at all like I thought babies were. She had pretty blond hair, just all pink and nice. And the doctor cleaned her eyes and nose and tied her cord. And he just lifted her up and held her out to me. "Here." And I said, "Oh!" I sat up with her all night long.

It's such a fascinating thing to see a baby emerge. You'd think it might be repulsive, but it isn't. And I missed the afterbirth and all the bad parts. Jim had to go out in the backyard and dig a hole to bury the afterbirth. You have to bury it deep, because the dogs will dig it up if they smell it.

I stayed with Fran for a week. Then Ed came down and we both went back to Morton. By that time both of us wanted to get out of there, so he got work on the railroad in Tacoma and we came down here to live. It wasn't too long after that that I found out I was pregnant.

We didn't plan it, but I never did anything to prevent it. I just never thought about it. With Carl, he used the withdrawal system. And I went to bed with Ed just twice before we got married. You have to know him to understand that. He's a very shy person, not forward at all. That appealed to me, I guess. It must have.

I'll never forget that first apartment we had in Tacoma. It was really crummy. It was so cold. It was at the bottom of an old house, and it had great big high ceilings. You could *not* heat that place. There was an oil circulator, no furnace. We put blankets over the doors to shut off some of the rooms. It was cold and it wasn't that clean. The house was about ready to fall down, but we couldn't afford anything else, because Ed was just a laborer on the railroad. He was bringing home about two hundred and twenty dollars a month, and I think we paid sixty-five a month rent.

Eventually we did find another apartment. It wasn't bad. Three rooms and a bath in the upstairs of a big old house. I remember there was a wringer-type washer on the main floor, and I used to lug the laundry downstairs, pregnant and all. And then Ed's brother sold us a car, a thirty-nine Ford. Ed still didn't know how to drive, and I still didn't have a license, but I drove.

I think one of the downfalls of our marriage is that we were never alone. First, Ed's brother Tracy, who was in the Army, was transferred to Fort Lewis, and he came and lived with us. And then his younger brother Pat, who was twelve or thirteen, moved in with us. Everything was so busy all the time. We'd go over and play

234

pinochle with my grandma and my sister all the time, or Grandma and I would go over to Mom's in Bremerton and sit and play pinochle all night. Pretty soon it seemed like all Ed's brothers and his sister were living with us. We were never alone. And by the time we were, it was too late. Ed was a funny guy. He never said much. I don't think I had any clear idea of him.

The night Lisa was born we had gone over to Ed's mother's for dinner. She had Swiss steak, which I love, and I overate. We were starting to do the dishes, and I felt like I had to go to the bathroom. Then I felt water running down my leg, and I thought, "I didn't make it!" But I hadn't had any pains or anything, so I just asked Ed's mother if she had any Kotex. She got me some and we started to do the dishes. Then I started having some little cramps. We came out to the living room. I remember Pat was sitting in the rocking chair and Ed was on the davenport. I sat down and kind of groaned. Pat kept peeking round at me, trying to figure out what was going on, and Ed looked at me. His mother said the baby was going to be here that night. Then the pains got stronger, and we called a cab and went to the hospital. Ed was real nervous. He went home to change his clothes; he'd been working in his mother's yard all day and was real grubby. I guess he wanted to look nice at the hospital. It was really funny.

I don't remember much about that birth because I was all doped up. Lisa was born just before midnight on August twelfth, 1953. I was still in the hospital on our first wedding anniversary.

•   •   •

Barbara & Lisa: 1953

When I got home from the hospital, Tracy and Pat were living with us. Then Mary, Ed's fifteen-year-old sister, came to stay. We had an army cot in the kitchen for Mary; Pat and Tracy slept on couches in the living room; and me and Ed and Lisa slept in the bedroom. Then Ken, Ed's other brother, who was in the Navy, got transferred here. When Tracy got out of the Army and left, Ken came to live with us. It was just a big party all the time. And all I wanted was to be alone.

Ed and I were getting along pretty good except we never talked or anything. I just had to get out of that apartment. I wanted us to get a house so bad. I wanted the space, and just to have something of our own. It scared Ed, I think. He wasn't making much money and to buy a house was a lot of responsibility. But I told him it was either a house or I was leaving.

When Lisa was two or three months old I got a job as a bookkeeper at a grocery company. Ed's mom baby-sat for me; I'd drop Lisa off at her house on my way to work and pick her up on my way home. I really enjoyed that job. There were only three girls working there. The company roasted and canned coffee, and it just used to smell so good. We'd go up and drink coffee and talk to the guys who roasted it. I only worked there two or three months, and then the company went out of business. So I went to the Bank of California as a bookkeeper.

At home, Mary and I did the housework and most times the boys cooked. They were terrible cooks. Things just kept going, but there were times I was so frustrated I'd just go to the room where Lisa was sleeping and sit on the bed. Just to get away. I talked to Ed about all of them living with us, but they didn't have anyplace else to go. The boys were in the service, so they couldn't afford to live on their own. And Pat was

237

too young. Mary finally went back to Yakima because she had a boyfriend there, but we still had Pat and Ken.

Well, we finally did buy a house and moved in about a week before Lisa's second birthday. It was real nice, that house. You walked in, and there was just a big room across the front—living room, dining room and kitchen, no dividers. It was an old house with wood siding. The stairway came down and curved into the living room. It had a nice kitchen and a back porch, and two bedrooms upstairs. We didn't have any furniture, so we went down to a store and bought three rooms of furniture. I remember the dining table was slate gray formica, with black legs; and there were chrome chairs. The davenport was beige, and the back of it went down to make a bed. We had one brown chair to match it. And end tables and lamps. The bedroom set had a bookcase headboard, two night tables and a double dresser. I remember the drapery store across from our apartment had a sale on fabric, and I got this fabric with a leaf design in reds and oranges. It was fun furnishing the house. Eventually Ed tore town the old garage to put a patio in, and he found a trapdoor. We asked some of the neighbors what it was for, and they said it was used during Prohibition to make liquor. A lot of the houses around there had places like that.

One day I was looking through *American Home,* and they had a picture of this old bathroom that looked exactly like ours—before and after pictures. I showed it to the husband of this girl I worked with; he was a contractor and I did his books, so he did the work for us. It turned out real neat, just like the after picture. We put in a built-in tub, blue fixtures and white tiles with gold flecks; we built a cupboard at one end of the tub, all the way to the ceiling, and had all the towels in there. And we built a counter. And we put in a piece of ripple plastic at the end, so the toilet was hidden. It was really cute. We worked together, Ed and me, and I enjoyed it.

I thought if we got the house and had more room I wouldn't mind everyone living there. But more room didn't help, because I still had to do everybody's washing. Ken had a car accident and broke his ankle. He was laying around the house because he couldn't work. I *know* it was an accident, but it was just something else to bother the nerves.

Then I had a two-week vacation, so I took Lisa and went over to Yakima for a week to see my dad. Ed and I were going to go camping at Sun Lake the second week. But when I got over there I just thought, "I can't go back." When I was away from it, I knew I didn't want to go back. I just felt relieved. I had no idea I was going to do that before I went to Yakima. I had no idea. I don't think I knew how unhappy I was.

I called Ed and told him not to come over and get me, that I wasn't coming back. I couldn't really give him a reason why. He came right over the next day, and I couldn't pinpoint why I didn't want to go back. We talked to Dad and to my stepmother Ethel, and they tried to talk me into going back for Lisa's sake. And the more they talked, the more rebellious I got. I didn't want to go back.

I got a job working for my cousin in Yakima for a few weeks, and Ed would come over every weekend. We'd talk and talk and try to iron things out. It was the first time we ever sat down and talked, and we'd been married four years.

One of the things we talked about was his job. Because I was getting a little disappointed in him as a person. He never tried to get a promotion, because he was afraid he'd be laid off. And by this time I was making more money than him. So he said he would take the next step up—that's what they call it on the railroad. And he said he'd go back and get the kids out of the house so we could be alone. Dad and Ethel thought that's what we needed, to be alone. I guess I felt that all those people were my responsibility. I had this feeling of being smothered.

So I went back. And I walked in the door, and Ed's sister and her girl friend and their boyfriends and Pat and Ken were in the living room. They were all still in *my* house. I just went up to the bedroom and sat on the bed and cried.

The kids were gone the next day, but I was so mad they weren't already gone when I got back. And there was no food in the house. It must have been between paydays and his family had eaten what food there was and the bills were coming due and there was no money to replenish the food. It was the first time that had happened. It really scared me. We'd never been in that situation before. I guess it was because I wasn't there. I always budgeted carefully, made lists on the first and fifteenth of the month of what had to be paid, and when, and how much would be left over.

I got a job right away at the Pacific Bank near where we lived. For a year everything was all right. I felt really good with everyone gone. I'd clean the house and it would *stay* clean.

I got pregnant with Felicia three or four months after I got back. In those years birth control wasn't so big a thing, and I just never thought about it. I tried a diaphragm, but I couldn't use it. And Ed tried condoms, but I got infections from those. There didn't seem to be anything that worked, so we just stopped using anything. But I was kind of happy I was pregnant, because we were getting along real well then. I would ask Ed about the promotion once in a while, but he never tried for

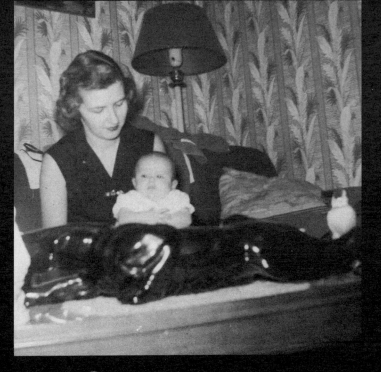

Barbara & Felicia: 1957

it. He'd say the railroad was getting ready for a layoff, and he'd lose his ten-year pension if he tried for a step up. That pension wasn't that important to me.

I guess my disappointment was building up during that time. He didn't change the way he said he was going to. He didn't take the next step up or go to night school. I guess I was growing up too.

Lisa was a good baby, the kind of kid who'd come back from the baby-sitter's looking just like she did when I left her there. I found this baby-sitter through the county. She had about nine kids in her house, some kids from welfare. The whole house was for kids. She was marvelous. She'd buy educational toys, and she even fed them breakfast. I only paid her two dollars a day.

I thought that when I had the other baby I'd be able to stay home. If Ed had taken the step up, his raise probably would have been enough for us to live on. I was looking forward to that, to staying home. And the pregnancy with Felicia was such a hard one. With Lisa I was just healthy all the time; I felt better than when I wasn't pregnant. With Felicia I used to pass out a lot. And I got so huge I couldn't see my toes. I didn't quit my job until I was about eight months pregnant.

Felicia was the most beautiful baby I ever saw. Olive skin, little penciled eyebrows, dark hair. She looked just like a little doll. She was very different from Lisa. Felicia was awkward. She'd take four steps and fall. And you couldn't keep her neat. If a drop of food got on Lisa's high chair, she'd start yelling for it to be cleaned up. It was funny, she couldn't stand to be messy.

Lisa and Felicia were both shy, but Felicia was terribly nervous. She was on tranquilizers when she was a baby. When she was real little she went into convulsions if you touched her. And I remember before she started school; she vomited for days, she was so scared about going.

I went back to work when Felicia was about four months old. I'd been in bookkeeping, but I went back as a teller. And then I went into the loan department as a secretary. By that time Ed was probably bringing home a hundred and sixty dollars every two weeks. I was making a lot more. I thought maybe that was part of the trouble between us. Grandma McCormack and my sister thought maybe it was too—that a wife shouldn't make more than her husband. They suggested I quit, but I couldn't quit altogether because I couldn't afford it. But I took a part-time job in a savings and loan company. I didn't tell Ed until I'd quit my job and gotten the other one. He didn't like it. I was only making enough to cover the bills. He didn't get mad, but he didn't like it.

I don't remember us ever really sitting down and talking. We didn't have any communication at all; that was our main problem, I think. Ed likes to talk to people but not get into things deeply. When we did have a spat he just quit talking. There'd be nothing said for days. I'd never known anyone like that. Especially a man. They usually blow up. But he just quit talking.

We were just drifting further apart. It got so I couldn't even stand for him to touch me. I'd cringe if he just touched my shoulder. If he went to bed, I'd stay up and watch the late late show. If he were watching it, I'd run up and go to sleep. That's a horrible way to live. We lived like that for a year or two.

Felicia was about two years old when he finally went to night school to learn

Barbara:
1952-1960

243

welding. But by that time things had really decayed. He started going hunting with his brothers on weekends, leaving me alone. And I started spending all my time at work, joining the Savings and Loan Institute, the Comptrollers Institute, things like that. They had meetings once a month; they gave classes and I took accounting. It was building up to where I didn't like to come home. And I'm sure it was the same for him.

Things just got worse and worse. Finally I told him I was taking my vacation and going to Yakima and that when I got back I wanted him to leave. We had a scene, but I think he knew I meant it. Things were so bad.

Dad was over in Yakima and so was Little Grandma. Dad didn't say anything when I told him. And Little Grandma, she didn't say too much either. Just that it was too bad. She never interfered. She had so many of us she just accepted whatever we did. I don't think she liked Ed, thought he was too quiet.

I had just made up my mind after all those years. You go through so much worry and heartache; and, with me, once I make up my mind, it's done. When I came back from Yakima I sold the house and moved back to Yakima. Felicia was going on four then; Lisa was about seven.

Barbara: 1960-1967

When I got back to Yakima I didn't have a job, but I wasn't worried about it. I knew I could get one. But almost right away I ran into Carl Eccles, my first boyfriend. He was out of the Army, recently divorced, working for the telephone company, installing switchboards. His wife had run off to Nevada with another guy, and Carl had his two boys with him. He wanted to marry me right away. I wanted to go slow, get a job, but his mother said, "Why? Why go to work?" We got married at his folks' house about a month after my divorce was final. That was October 1961. And it didn't work. It just didn't work from the very beginning.

When Carl was a kid, he was overpowering, a center-of-attraction type of person. At the time I thought it was so great, that he was so good at everything. And his parents and grandparents had been so good to me; they'd kept in touch all those years. When Lisa was born his mother even made some booties and a little hat for her. That's why, when I remet Carl, I wanted to go back with him. Because he was my first love. But I didn't stop to know him. When you're older you don't look at things the same way. He was really a kind of braggart. Everything he did, he thought he did a little better than anyone else. And he had to be catered to.

I didn't go to work after we were married. I had bought a house in Yakima, and he and his boys moved in there. His boys were spoiled rotten. The oldest was Felicia's age, the other was a year and a half younger. They couldn't tie their shoelaces or button their coats. They'd been without their mother for six or seven months.

245

At first I guess things were okay between us. He was good with my kids and we'd do things together, like go fishing. Then, after a little while, he didn't want to take the kids when we went someplace. I should have realized that his parents really ran his life—everything was to please them. Like I joined this women's group with his mother—the Junior Women's Club. We made clothes for the hospital; we worked with mentally retarded children, made bandages. I enjoyed it; it was really rewarding doing that type of thing. To me, Carl would complain about my doing all those projects; but when he talked to his parents he'd say he was really proud of me.

Later I found out that he treated the kids differently; when I went out to meetings he'd send the girls up to bed and keep the boys up. And he got mean. He was drinking really badly. Several times when we were supposed to go over to his parents I had to call up and say that he or I was sick. Because of the booze. And he beat the boys. Over little things, nothing. And when we'd go to his parents they'd make such a fuss over the boys, and the girls would just go off in the corner. My girls were withdrawing; I just couldn't see that happening. I begged him to talk to his parents about treating the kids equally, but he never did. His grandpa, the one I had lived with, saw what was happening, and he was really good with the girls. They loved going over there. He was the only one who treated all the kids the same.

I tried so hard with the boys, but David, the oldest, built up this hatred of me because I was the disciplinarian. The teacher at school told me, just before Carl and I separated, that David was starting to straighten out, and he was showing affection for me in his drawings and things. It was sad because I tried so hard.

Carl had changed so much. He'd gone through the service and a marriage. I expected him to be the same. And he was different. And I was different. Like he had a permit for a gun, and when he wanted to show off when we went someplace, he wore his gun and holster. That was really embarrassing to me.

When I got pregnant we thought it might bring the family together. That was a miserable pregnancy. I had heartburn the whole time—it didn't matter what I ate. If I lay down it was really painful, so I ended up sitting in a chair all night. I was working really hard then, remodeling the house. And I'd be reading and get a blind spot so I couldn't see, like I had blinders on. One day I started to go to the bathroom and I couldn't see at all. It just lasted a couple of minutes, but it scared me to death. From then on I never went anyplace without Lisa or Felicia, so in case something went wrong they could call for help.

When Jenny was born, his boys rejected her completely. They said she was my baby, not theirs. So the idea of bringing the family together didn't work at all.

About six months after Jenny was born I went back to work. I got a job at United Builders, doing closings on houses. Carl was working nights then and I was working days. It was sometime soon after I got that job that Kennedy was killed. I remember they closed the office really early that day and everybody just went home and watched TV. Everything kind of stopped moving. The funeral was really terrible. The kids, Felicia especially, were just sitting there crying. I don't know what it was about Kennedy. It was funny that feeling he gave you when he talked. It was like he wasn't talking politics; he was talking to *you* about the troubles of the country. I really believed in him. I don't know if it was his personality or the fact that he was a younger

Barbara:
1960-1967

247

man and appealed more to younger people. But he seemed more like an everyday type person, somebody who wanted to fight for the smaller person. But, really, he started all the integrated schools that caused so much trouble. It could have been handled differently, I think; he rushed into it too fast. And everybody was really scared during the missile crisis. The Russians were ready to fire missiles at us and we were ready to fire at them. It was just a standoff.

I was out duck hunting with my father-in-law when his assassinator was killed. We had stopped at this friend's house; and we were sitting there having a cup of coffee, warming up, and it came on TV. It was all so unbelievable. The whole thing. That somebody really killed the President.

I always thought that Mrs. Kennedy was so pretty. She wasn't really, but she was a striking woman. Very elegant. It didn't matter if she was in her riding habit or blue jeans or what. She was just elegant. When she married Onassis it seemed like she was doing something against the American people.

The whole thing was so terrible. It was like losing someone of your own when he was killed. I think maybe I felt even worse about it because, by that time, I knew pretty well what I was going to do. I couldn't take any more with Carl.

When I was at work the baby-sitter told me how Carl would come in the back door, fix himself a big drink, go out the front door and come in the back for another drink again. He did that all day long. One night Jenny had a really bad cold, and I was sleeping in her room because I was worried. He came in and held his forty-five pistol to my head and he said, "I should kill you." I said, "Fine. Go ahead if it makes you feel better," and he cocked the pistol. I just lay there. I didn't think he'd do anything and he didn't. He turned around and left the room. I found out later that he used to do that to his ex-wife all the time.

I didn't talk to him about a divorce. I just went to a lawyer and filed papers and had them served on him at work. I was scared of him. After I had the papers served he wasn't allowed to come to the house, so his dad came and got his things and the boys' things. One night, though, Carl came to the door and said he wanted some of the boys' stuff. I told him he couldn't come in the house. Then he said he wanted to see Jenny, and I said I'd bring her out. But he pushed his way onto the back porch. He picked up a baseball bat. And I picked up a frying pan. After that I packed up the kids and went to Mom's. She had an apartment in downtown Yakima then, and I called his dad from there and told him Carl had threatened me. He said not to worry, it wouldn't happen again. I called my attorney and he called the sheriff, and I didn't have any trouble with him after that. Carl had been pretty good with Jenny, but after I filed for divorce he never saw her again, never even tried.

I don't know. Maybe if we'd waited before we got married, gotten to know each other, let the kids get to know each other and us, it would have been all right. Maybe. I don't know. Neither Mom or Grandma McCormack liked him. I thought I loved him, and the first year we were married wasn't really that bad. But I think my feelings were left over from high school days.

I felt bad about the divorce. I felt like a real loser. And I really dug into my job and the club work and the kids. I kept myself busy. The Junior Women's Club had meetings once a month, and then smokers maybe once a week, to do the project we were working on. I had three or four girl friends, and if I started getting depressed I'd call one of them and we'd go and do something. You learn how to train yourself out of it when you feel a depression coming on. As long as I was busy, I was all right. You need close girl friends to talk to, especially when the kids are little. It was so much harder then; now I've got Felicia and Lisa to talk to, but then when I got depressed a girl friend and I would sit and talk or take the kids to the show or get a baby-sitter and have our hair done, usually some dumb thing like that. Once we went over and started painting my girl friend Liz's house because we didn't have anything else to do.

I only met Liz's husband twice. Mike was his name. He was in the Marines, in Vietnam. He'd been over to Vietnam four or five different times, and she showed me his letters about what was happening over there. The first time or two he was there, the villagers were pretty good, he said. The guys took a lot of little Vietnamese kids to their camp, and they'd feed them and play games with them. Mike went back when his tour was over because he really wanted to help. He'd gotten to know a lot of natives through the little kids. But the last couple of times he went there, he wrote that the people were all different. You couldn't have the little kids around, because they'd steal you blind. Or you wouldn't know if they had grenades under their clothes and would blow you and half the men in the camp up. Horrible. Little kids! And women! They'd have to strip the women down, and they'd find ammunition and stuff underneath their dresses, all tied around them. It was like the people were fighting against them too. They couldn't trust anybody anymore.

I didn't really blame our servicemen when I heard about My Lai. From what Mike wrote about the villagers—he'd say how they'd go into villages and the people would run from them and they'd find munitions in their huts. And they'd help the Cong, give food to the Cong, but they wouldn't help us. And we were over there to help them. I can see how these guys would get so bitter against those people.

I never did understand about Vietnam. Everybody was saying: Here we go into another Korea. But we didn't make any progress. We'd burn the jungle out so the Vietcong couldn't use it, but by doing that we took away all the livelihood of the villagers. It didn't make sense to me. I couldn't make out what they were really fighting for. I don't think we'll ever know the true story about it. Nothing happened in Yakima about that. I mean, there weren't any protest demonstrations or anything. I guess that people just felt that they didn't know the whole story and that the people who were running things did. I didn't really think about it too much. I was just thinking about getting along.

I didn't have very much money. I had to get a second job, at night, part time, because we were short of money. I couldn't do for the kids what I would have liked to do. Carl was paying fifty dollars a month for Jenny, but Ed never paid anything for Lisa and Felicia. I went to the prosecutor a couple of times when things got really bad and I needed money at school time, but Ed didn't have it, so it never did much good. He was struggling too. He had married and had little kids. I kind of felt sorry for him. I knew I could get by; it wasn't that bad, although at times I thought it was.

I didn't like to think about what would happen if I got sick or lost my job. When I'd get depressed I'd think about things like that. But I thought, "Other people make

Barbara:

1960-1967

it; I'll worry about it when the time comes." What depressed me most was being alone and thinking about the years going by. What was going to happen to me? To the kids?

I couldn't afford to have a baby-sitter come to the house after I separated from Carl, so I took the kids to the mother of one of Lisa's friends. She had three older girls, so if she couldn't sit, one of her girls would. And the kids were just like part of her family. The high school cheerleaders made Jenny a mascot when she was two. I took her to all the games, and she had a cheerleading outfit and used to do the splits and all the cheers by herself. We had a lot of fun with her. She was a real active kid. I can see a lot of Lisa's personality in Jenny—mainly stubbornness and always wanting to know "Why?" Felicia was different; you just told her this or that, and that was it.

When Lisa and Felicia were younger, I was always tense, afraid that they would get hurt. But I was more relaxed with Jenny. I believe you've got to teach kids when they're young and leave them alone later. When Jenny was about three months old she could push herself backwards and forwards in the walker; I had knickknacks all around, and when she touched them I slapped her hands purple. Mom used to get so mad at me. "Just pick her up," she'd say. And Dad used to get upset when he saw it. But it didn't take Jenny long to learn not to touch things.

Mom came to stay with me just after the divorce. She had a terrible gall stone operation and she couldn't work for about three months, so she came and baby-sat until she went back to work. We had a real big house then, four bedrooms, two baths, four acres of land. And it was four or five miles out of town. It was just too expensive for me to keep going. I sold it and rented a repossessed house real cheap. But I didn't like renting. It's just not the same as when it's your own. I think that's a throwback to when I was a kid and we rented all the time and moved all the time. I wanted something permanent for the kids.

Then, at United Builders, where I was working, the guy who had my job before me wanted to come back. So, in effect, they demoted me and lowered my wages. I said, "No, I won't take that." And I quit. I really shocked myself. Here I was supporting a family, and I quit a job. But I got another job, at a mortgage company, right away.

Really, things weren't bad. I had my kids, my job and the Women's Club. Every Thursday night I went bowling with my girl friends. We used to giggle and laugh and didn't care if we won or lost. My girl friend Doreen was on the team, and on weekends the kids and I would go out to her ranch. The kids would ride horses and run around and have a good time.

The next fall, after the divorce, two couples invited me to a football game, and I met the first fellow I went out with after the divorce. He was a schoolteacher, really nice. He was real good with Jenny; he wouldn't let us talk baby-talk to her, and she learned to talk quick. I went out with him for about six or seven months and we had a lot of fun. His folks had a big ranch in the valley and he had a Honda there. He'd take the kids for rides on it; then we'd go up riding in the hills for an hour or two while his mom baby-sat. There wasn't any real love involved in it. Just enjoyment. We had a lot of friends in common, gals from the club and people we went to school with. We went together all through the winter, and the holiday season. It was really good for me, something I needed. It brought me out of being tied down with the kids, and yet we

Barbara:
1960-1967

253

included the kids a lot. It was just a nice relationship. Then we drifted apart. It just happened, no big deal. I didn't feel badly.

But Yakima's not an easy town to live in if you're single. It's a little town, and the people can be little. I remember one night when Jenny was a baby, my dad came and stayed with me. He left about four in the morning to go fishing. The next night was really hot, and Lisa and I went out on the front porch to get a little breeze. The neighbors across the street had some people over, and when they were leaving I heard her telling them how I'd had a man stay with me the night before and what a terrible woman I was. That's the way the town was. It didn't matter what you did; someone made something of it. I told the kids one time: I don't care if I do stay out all night or some guy brings me home and he's too drunk to go home so he sleeps on the couch. As long as you know what I'm doing, I couldn't care what the rest of the world thinks.

Of course there were nice things about living in a small town, too. There was another lady who was always rescuing Jenny out of a tree and giving the kids cookies, and they'd make things for her and leave them on her front porch.

I finally quit the Women's Club. I just kind of drew away from it. They were so good to me after the divorce, making me chairman of this and that—which was what I needed. But it was all married couples and I felt out of place. I joined the Insurance Women's Club and went to night school and took real estate law. I was working in mortgages, and all I knew about it was what I had picked up along the way, so I enjoyed learning more. And you meet a lot of different people. I had some friends who were really good to me. On Thanksgiving and Christmas and family-type holidays they'd include us in their families. Those special days are really hard when you're

Barbara, Lisa, & Jenny: 1967

single. Dad had left Yakima by then; he was over in Tacoma. And Grandma McCormack was over there, too. Mom was in Yakima; she'd spend holidays with Little Grandma and Uncle Charlie. I guess I would rather have been with my friends than with them.

Mom was living on the other side of Yakima from me. One time I got sick, and the doctor told me I had pneumonia and I had to go to the hospital. I said, "I can't! I've got three kids and a couple of cats and a dog, and I can't go to the hospital." So he said, "Then you have to go home and go to bed. You can't get up." I said, "What are you talking about? I can't do that!" And he said I had to.

I went over to the baby-sitter's to get Jenny, and I just broke down and cried and cried. She said, "Leave Jenny here and go home and go to bed." When I went home I called Mom and asked her if she'd come out and fix the kids' dinners. She said, "No." I said, "Why not?" And she said it was too hard to get back and forth. She wouldn't come.

Lisa was in the seventh grade then, and Felicia was in the fifth. It was Lisa that took care of me. She came home at noon and fixed me bouillon, really doing a beautiful job taking care of me. My dad called after I'd been sick for about a week, not knowing I was sick. When I told him he said he'd take his vacation and come over. But I said I'd be all right now. It's really a disheartening thing. There was just never anybody to help when I really needed it. You think there should be somebody, but there never is. You've just got to take care of yourself. You can get really down, and I used to get down. But you always make it through.

Barbara: 1967-1974

I met Roger at the Insurance Institute. A judge had come to speak there and nine of us took him to a cocktail lounge afterwards. Roger was with a fellow we all knew. He didn't make any impression on me at all. In fact, we left the lounge and went to a place to dance. Roger asked me to dance and I didn't want to. He started phoning me and finally I went out with him. I think it was January 1967 I met him.

We had a nice relationship the first couple of months. He wasn't the pushy kind sexually, or wanting to neck. He liked to sit and just talk. We'd talk about the kids and work. He'd been divorced and had two daughters. He had his own wholesale grocery business and traveled a lot.

He was possessive, I guess you'd call it. One night, after we'd gone out together about three or four times, he called me and asked me to come to this cocktail lounge where we always went. I said I'd come and have one drink, but that I would have to go back to work. So I met him there and then I said I had to be going. He said he did too. About an hour later the kids called me at work to say Roger called home to see if I was there. He was afraid I'd lied to him. I didn't mind it. I was flattered.

We'd been going out for about five months when I had to go to the hospital for a D & C. Roger said he'd stay with the kids over that weekend. He came to see me in the hospital, stayed for about five minutes and then he said he had to leave. I found out later that he took some other girl out all weekend. I was just floored. So I told him, "Fine, if that's what you want to do, I won't stand in your way." Because he was recently divorced and I figured he wanted to kick up his heels. But I was upset. I said, "Go, I don't need you that badly." But he wouldn't stay away. He kept coming around, saying that he loved me but that he just had to get out. And I'd say, "Okay, get out. Don't bother me." But he'd keep coming over to the house, stay for two or three hours and then leave to go out. Finally I said, "Leave us alone completely. It's too upsetting."

I had stopped almost everything I did to be with him. I had been seeing him almost every night, and so I had to try to start everything up again real quick. I started bowling and going around with the group I used to. Then, about two or three weeks later, I was at this bar we all went to and Roger called there and asked me to come over to his house. He said, "Please," so I went, and he said he'd been doing some thinking. He wanted to marry me. I didn't know what to say at first. Then I realized he really did love me, and I said, "Yes."

Things were pretty stormy after that. We'd have fights, and he'd walk out and then come back so sorry and say, "I love you." I used to get so depressed I would just sit around and cry because he'd make me feel bad. He was so jealous. Now, I'd been single for three years, and I'd had a few boyfriends. If we went someplace and saw a man I knew, Roger'd say, "Oh, is that one of your old boyfriends?" And we'd have a fight. But I figured things would settle down after we were married.

We had a real big wedding in the Lutheran church. First, we had counseling with the pastor, and he talked to us about what we wanted in our lives and were we sure about getting married. The kids and I got baptized.

Dad gave me away at the wedding. It was the first time he'd done that. Everything seemed to be the way it should be. The whole family was there—Mom and Grandma McCormack and Little Grandma. Doreen was matron of honor. I wore a blue sheath with a net overskirt I'd made, and we had a big reception afterwards. Dad and Ethel took the kids, and we came over to Tacoma for the weekend for a honeymoon. These friends of Roger's had a big trailer, and we stayed with them. And we went to two or three nice places in Seattle. It was all real nice.

After we got back to Yakima I went back to work. I was in the loan department at the bank, and it was a responsible position. You had to be available if work had to be done, and sometimes I had to work late. Roger didn't like that. I was *his*. He wanted me to quit, but we couldn't afford that. He'd quit his own business by then and was working for a wholesale grocery company; then he started working as a bartender part-time. Finally he quit the grocery business altogether. He said it was too confining.

Until I married Roger I never completely trusted anybody. I never let anybody dominate my life, because it scared me. I always kept something of myself. I worked and belonged to clubs. I always had a little bit that was my own thing. But when I married Roger I gave it all up. He made me feel guilty for wanting to do anything on my own, and I accepted it. If I worked late at the bank, he thought I was going out or having a party. He'd make me feel like I was doing something wrong. After we got married I never went out to see Doreen, and the kids and I used to go out there every weekend. And I used to bowl once a week, but I had to quit because he didn't like to bowl, and why did I need to go bowl with the women? It was such a gradual thing I didn't realize it until everything was gone. It's funny how you can get yourself into a trap like that and you don't realize it until it's happened, it's done. And then you don't know what to do about it.

He was just afraid all the time. He would always accuse me of going out—which I didn't. If I was half an hour late from work: "Where've you been?" If I wanted to go out to Doreen's: "What do you want to go *there* for?" If we ran into some man I knew: "Where do you know *him* from?" He always used to get me so mixed up. He'd put me down and make me feel like I'd done something wrong. If I was cooking, he'd come out and start adding things to it. If I'd say, "Don't do that, *I'm* cooking it," he'd say "Well, you're not doing it right." And then I'd get upset, and he'd say I was stupid to make such a scene over it. "That's such a dumb thing to be upset about. Are you going crazy?" He would twist things around so it would be my fault, and I'd give in to him.

Then he wanted to go to Alaska. He made it seem like everything would be different if we went. We'd have all new friends, an all new life. There were too many old memories in Yakima, old girl friends, old boyfriends. I tried to talk him out of it. I kept telling him that you can't run away from problems. "If we're going to have problems we'll have them anywhere," I said. But he decided that if we were up there, we could start over.

We went up to Alaska the May after we were married. Lisa came with us; Felicia and Jenny stayed down to finish the year in school. We rented the house in Yakima and just took blankets, dishes, whatever we could fit in the car. When we got up to Anchorage we rented an apartment. Roger got a job the next day as a bartender at a

Lisa, Felicia, & Jenny: 1968

cocktail lounge. I got a job two days later at the National Bank of Alaska. He worked nights and I worked days.

We'd been up there a month when he beat me up. He picked me up from work one day and he started in on me. Out of the clear blue sky he said I was a rotten person. "What did *I* do?" Well, you've been out with men and you did this and that. And I said, "I was free and single and I could do what I felt like doing. What I did before I met you is none of your business. If you don't like it, that's too bad."

He was still going on when we got home. Lisa shut herself in her room because she didn't want to listen to him. I went and sat in the kitchen to write a letter, and he was sitting in the living room drinking, ranting, you know. I just sat there writing my letter and pretty soon he came out. He couldn't stand that I wouldn't fight back. He grabbed me and started banging me against the refrigerator. He grabbed me around the neck and I couldn't even scream. It was just unbelievable. The only reason he probably didn't kill me was that Lisa came up behind him and was hitting him on the back, screaming, *"I hate you. I hate you."* That shocked him and he let go of me and knocked her across the room. Then, all of a sudden, he must have realized what he had done, and left. It's really terrible to have a man beat you. You think you can stop him, but you can't do a thing.

Lisa and I just packed up and left. I came down the Alcan Highway just, oh, in really bad shape. But a month later I went back to him. Roger was the only one of my husbands I loved. Ed was too quiet. And I don't count Carl; that was on the rebound; I just wanted something with him I'd once had before. I guess I loved Roger because he dominated me. I must have wanted that. I really cared what he thought. I would have done anything for him. But he went too far. I never got to go to my dad's funeral because of Roger.

My dad and I had got real close again, back to our old relationship. One day, it was after Jenny was born, we just sat down and talked. We got everything out into the open. I told him how I felt when he and Mom separated and why I left when I was living with him. And he said how bad he had felt about my leaving, but he was so wrapped up in himself then, he really couldn't think about me. We had a good understanding after that. He was always there when I needed him. You keep these hidden resentments toward people, you don't let them show; but they're there and it keeps you from having the relationship you should have.

After I married Roger we found out Dad had cancer. He had an operation, and they found a cancer in his lung the size of a softball. The doctor said, "Don't worry, I got it all." But after Roger and I went to live in Alaska my sister called and said Dad was dying. "He's just waiting for you" is the way she put it.

Of course we didn't have a dime; no money for me to get back. But I told my boss, and he said, "Of course you're going home," and he charged the ticket to the office. I flew down to Tacoma on the eighteenth of December.

Dad looked awful. So thin. Nothing but skin and bones. I went to the hospital every day and sat with him, fed him. My stepmother, Ethel, was there day and night, and I spelled her so she could go home and take a nap. They had Dad in a very small room and he got claustrophobic. At first we thought he was choking. We'd hold him up and raise the window, but it didn't help. He was an outdoor man, he'd always worked outdoors, and he couldn't stand being in such a small room.

So I had them move him into a bigger room. They wheeled him down the hall and I held his hand. He always wanted you to hold his hand. He knew he was dying. He was in terrible pain. His head would hurt so bad. Ethel didn't like to ask for pain pills; she's a terribly religious person, and she and Dad would pray together. But I couldn't stand to see him in pain, so when she'd leave I'd call the nurse and get a pain shot for him.

My plane reservations back to Alaska were for the night of the twenty-third. Dad said, "You have to go, don't you?" I said, "Yeah, I have to have Christmas with the kids. I don't want them to be alone." He started to say something, but I couldn't understand him. I told him he could tell me later. He started to go to sleep, and then my cousin came in. Dad heard his voice and said hello and asked about his mother. Then he started having pain. I told my cousin to leave and stop at the nurse's desk to ask for a pain shot. Then Dad turned on his side and took my hand in both of his and went to sleep. The nurse came in to give him the shot, and I said, "I don't think he'll need it now. He's going to sleep." She looked at him and said, "He's dead."

He just lay there and died. Oh *God*. I always cry when I talk about this. I never got to cry then. I started to cry when the nurse told me. She took me out of the room, and I saw my brother-in-law coming down the hall. There was nothing I wanted more than for him to—you know, put his arms around me so I could cry. But he didn't. He just stood there. Nobody's ever done that for me. All I wanted was to be able to cry for my dad, and there was too much to do.

Ethel came back, and the minute she got off the elevator she knew there was something wrong. I had to take her into an empty room till she calmed down a little bit and they'd had a chance to straighten Dad up. She went in and sat with him for a little while, and when she came out everyone was just standing around. Everybody was just hanging on me: What are we going to do? What are we going to do? So I had to make all these decisions. First I told my brother-in-law to take Ethel back to his house, because she didn't want to go home. Then I took his car and went to tell my sister's kids. And I called Fran's boss—she was working as a checker at the Safeway—and asked him to get her out of the checkstand when he saw us coming. When Fran saw me, she looked at her watch and said, "You guys are early." Then she saw my face and really broke up. We had to take her in the back room for a while.

And then there were my dad's clothes. Ethel couldn't go in the house by herself to get them, so I had to go in. My sister stood on the curb and got hysterical. Then we had to go to the funeral parlor and make all the arrangements. And we had a terrible time arranging to move Dad's body to Yakima on the train; he got to ride free because he'd worked on the railroad.

I made so many phone calls that night. I can't remember how many. I called Roger and told him Dad had just died. And he said, "Well, you knew it would happen." I said that I wanted to stay for the funeral, and he said, "What do you want to stay for? He's dead." My God!

I only stayed until all the arrangements were made. I had to give the funeral director all the information to put in the paper, and he was going to put down that my brother was dad's stepson. I knew Dad wouldn't want that, because he'd raised Bill ever since he was tiny. Ethel said, "I suppose we have to do it that way," and I said,

Barbara, her father, & Fran: ca. 1958

"No! You just put down that he was survived by his son and two daughters, and put their names. I don't care if the names are the same or not."

I didn't want to do all this stuff. I just wanted to sit back and cry. Everybody always thought I was so secure in myself, I was so strong. And *I* needed help.

They had the funeral the day after Christmas, and then they took Dad back to Yakima and had services for him there too because he had a lot of friends there. I wanted to stay really bad. People say funerals are a bad thing, but they're not. They're a place to go and cry. You get all the emotion out. If you don't go, it stays inside you. I always resented Roger for that, for not letting me stay.

I don't know why I didn't stay anyway. I guess I was afraid of him. He had me so down I was crying all the time. Nothing I did was right. I didn't keep the house right. I didn't cook right. I didn't dress right. And if I'd say something, it wasn't the right thing. When I'd try to talk to him about it, he'd twist it around so it was all my fault. He'd tell me I was going crazy, and I thought maybe I was. You really can be brainwashed.

I left him again and came back down to Yakima with the kids. I got a job and a house and I was feeling real good. I liked the way I felt, being away from him. And yet I still wanted to be with him. I still loved him. I don't understand it myself, but that's the way it was. He came down from Alaska in July, but I didn't see him until September. When I saw him again I turned around and let him come back. And everything started all over again. I ended up quitting my job at the bank and we went to work together in a restaurant. Roger was the bartender and I helped in the kitchen and worked in the cocktail lounge on weekends. That was fun. We met a lot of nice people and there wasn't the mental strain I had working in the bank. Roger and I got along well working together, which was strange. We just had a good time. At work, anyway. Then, in February, he was arrested.

It must have been about three-thirty in the afternoon. I was home sick when the police came to the house. They asked me where our car was. I said my husband had it but he'd be home soon because he had to go to work. I said, "Why don't you come in?" And they said, "We'll just wait outside." I didn't know what to think. I guess I thought Roger had run a light, or something like that.

Roger pulled in and I saw the police go over to talk to him. Then another police car went by with some little kids in it. I thought, "What's going *on* here?" The police left, and Roger came in and said that the cops thought they saw the car up at the high school and they were looking for a dope pusher. He had to go over to the police station the next morning and clear it up. All that night he lay in bed sweating. The whole bed was sopping wet.

The next morning he left to go down to the courthouse. I didn't hear from him all day, and I was getting upset because it was getting on to four o'clock and we usually left then to go to work. The phone rang. He said, "I'm in jail." I thought he was drunk and he was joking. He said, "No, I'm in jail." "What are you *talking* about?" I said. He said, "Well, I got caught. Bring me down some clothes to go to court with tomorrow and I'll tell you."

I called the detectives and they told me what had happened. Some kids at the school had reported that a man was trying to pick them up. They'd seen the car up there before, but this time a teacher had taken down the license number. She'd seen him trying to pick up some little kids. He didn't actually ever have intercourse with the kids—just exposure and showing dirty pictures. Oh, God, what a *shock!*

It's pretty weird seeing policemen lead your husband into court and hearing him sentenced to twenty years. I went to talk to him afterwards. He said he hoped I'd understand. I didn't understand *anything.*

I didn't know what to do. I went home and called Mom. She wasn't home. I called my aunt. She wasn't in either. I wanted somebody to help me, but what could anyone do?

The court recommended they send Roger to this hospital for observation. They had a program there for sex offenders, and if they feel they can help them, they take them in. So I moved the kids over there, outside Tacoma. What could I do? I tried to understand. The doctors said it had to do with being afraid of grown women. But I never noticed anything. Nothing. Up there at the hospital I'd talk to the other wives, and you wouldn't believe the things that went on—incest and stuff, and the wives never knew anything about it. The doctors told me that was why Roger behaved the way he did to me. That the reason he always told me I was a rotten person was because he felt he was so rotten himself, and he had to switch it over to me, blame everything on me.

That business with Roger really ran me down. I was sick when he was arrested, and after that I got pneumonia again and couldn't work. The doctor said I needed a complete rest. I had no money; Roger was in that hospital. I had to go on welfare. I've had two jobs sometimes, just to support the kids. I've always been so strong and done everything for the kids and taken care of myself. And here I was on welfare. How low can any man sink you?

I went on welfare in March 1970 and didn't go back to work until the following January. I got a hundred and thirty dollars a month, but my house rent was ninety-five. It was rough. It was really depressing. The caseworker came around once in a while, and I had to go down to the office to get food stamps. I paid sixty dollars for one hundred dollars' worth of stamps. It was the most degrading thing. First you have to sign this slip, and then you wait for them to call you. Sometimes you sit there all day long. One day I sat next to two winos. And the little kids. They're just filthy. I don't care if you *are* on welfare, you don't have to be dirty. It would make you vomit. And it's degrading, going to the store and paying with the stamps. You have to separate everything because they won't take stamps for toilet paper or soap.

Roger was in the hospital for nineteen months. I stuck with him all that time. I'd visit him on Saturday nights, take meals up there because he didn't like the cooking, go to the marriage group on Thursdays. But Roger always told me to watch what I said to the doctors and the other group members. He said to keep everything light, not to tell about our problems or get involved. The doctors said he was supposed to be learning to control his fantasies and behavior patterns; he was a borderline psychopath, they said. They were so matter-of-fact about it. To them it was such a trivial thing.

After nineteen months he got on a work-release program, and then they started letting him come home on weekends. He came home for good in August, and then he was on probation till June. He was really good then. He used to take us places and be nice to me and the kids. Then, as soon as the parole was over, he changed again. He started being really mean, putting me down, yelling at me over everything.

It was my third marriage. You hate to give up the third time around. Roger said what we needed was to have a baby. It would give us a new start. I said we were too old. I didn't want to, I really didn't. I'd been on the pill, and Roger had a fit when he found out. If I was nervous or upset, he'd blame it on the pill. So I went off it. He said he'd use contraceptives, but he didn't. So of course I got pregnant.

One day I was ironing, and he just started in yelling at me. I can't remember why. He said, "What's the matter with *you?*" As if there was something wrong with *me!* And I finally said, "Leave me *alone!* I'm *pregnant.* That's what you *wanted,* isn't it?"

We were living in Tacoma when Ian was born; we were getting along terribly. Roger used to say we should sit down and talk about things. So I'd say, "Well, you said this, or that, and it really upset me." He'd say, "Why?" And I'd say, "Because it put me down, made me feel bad." Then he'd say, "Well, you *shouldn't* feel that way."

I should never feel the way I felt. It would always end up in a big fight because he would never listen to the way I felt. It got to the point where I thought maybe I didn't really feel the way I felt.

One night we were out at the Harbor Lights, which is a restaurant here, and everybody was having a really good time. I went to the rest room, and when I came back to the bar Roger turned around and said, "Here's that bitch." I said, *"What?"* I didn't know what was wrong; he would just change that quick. To get out of the restaurant I had to go through the kitchen, and climb over a fence because it was after hours and they had the front door locked. I walked home and packed all his clothes. He had a lot of clothes—two suitcases and six boxes of his clothes. I was thinking how just two months before I had bought some clothes for forty dollars and he started yelling. But he could spend that for just a shirt, slacks and a tie.

When he came home that night he slept in the basement, and the next day I told him to go. He started to hit me in the face. I said, "My God, don't hit me in the face. I've got to go to work." That's all I could think of. If he hit me in the face I wouldn't be able to go to work. I guess it dawned on him that if he did, everybody would know. So he just kicked my body. The only reason he left was Felicia tried to call the police. He grabbed the phone from her and was going to hit her with it. I jumped between them and made her go out the back door, over to the neighbor's. Then I tried to get out the back door, and he dragged me back by my hair. Just horrible. But, after that, I was finished with him.

I dragged the kids through a lot in those years. Lisa couldn't stand living with Roger. She went to live with her father for a while and I was pretty bitter about that. I depended on Lisa for a lot. "After all I've done for her, she's leaving," I thought. "After as hard as I worked." But she just couldn't stand the way it was in the house. After the way he beat me in Alaska and his being arrested and the way he'd gotten me so beat down, I wasn't a person anymore. I just did everything he wanted, and Lisa thought I didn't have to go along with him. Before she left we'd get in big fights because she was always in her room; she'd come home from school and go to her room, eat and go to her room. I don't think she really hated me. Maybe it felt like hate at the

Barbara, Ian, & Hannah: 1973

Jenny,
Barbara,
Jan, & Felicia: 1973

time, but hate is a different thing. She didn't understand. I felt I *had* to keep trying with Roger. I had to keep trying until I gave up. Otherwise I would blame myself too much. You think of how many times you've been married. Three times. And people say, "Oh, you really go through the men, don't you?" I had to try the hardest I could. But I can understand what Lisa felt.

She called me after she'd been at her dad's three or four months and asked if she could come home. I said, "Fine, your room's always here." That was in May, I think, and she and Tony got married a few months later. That wedding was really something. When I saw her walking down the aisle, I just started sobbing. From way, way down. These big spasms. It was my baby getting married.

Lisa was eighteen when she got married. She and Tony had been going together since they were in eighth grade, so I expected it. She was old enough to make her own decisions. But when Felicia wanted to get married she was real young—sixteen. I could have said no, but then I thought she might have turned against me. She did a lot of talking about it and I'd go along with her, but if she'd started making definite plans I think I would have stopped it. But she stopped it on her own. She was real moody for three or four weeks, and one day I sat her down at the table and asked her what the problem was. She said, "Nothing, just nothing." And then she started crying and said that she just didn't think she really wanted to get married, but everybody knew about it already. And I said, "Who cares what other people think? It's better now than to be married two years and divorced. Your life's your own. Don't let other people lead it." I used to worry so much about whether people liked me. It takes a lot to outgrow that.

That's probably why I had three bad marriages. Because I was looking for something from someone else. A lot of my insecurity I'm sure came from Mom. Because Mom was so insecure, and still is. It can't help but rub off.

Mom and Grandma don't talk about personal things very much. Which is too bad because maybe if they'd talked about them, it would have been better. One time Mom was over here, and we were watching a show on TV where a woman leaves her husband and kids and goes off to find herself by herself. The little kid on the show, it really hurt him when his mother left; and the older kids didn't understand it. Mom said, "That woman really needed to get away." And I said, "I don't see how she could walk away and leave her kids. My kids are my responsibility and I love them. I just couldn't stand to be away from them; they're part of me." And Mom said, "Yeah, I guess you're right."

It made me think how she'd done the same thing. If she could just talk about it—but she won't ever. I've never really tried to make her, because she gets mad really easily and it's real hard for her to get over being mad. And maybe I don't really want to talk about it, either. I just figure it's best left unsaid. It's too easy to hurt people and get yourself hurt.

Mom's been pretty good lately, in the last few years. I don't think she's drinking so much, on account of her ulcer. She just worships Ian, and I have her baby-sit once in a while—she likes the responsibility. I see her about every week or two. I don't want her to get dependent on me. I'd like her to get out and do something on her own, but I don't think she's going to do it. I worry about her. I worry that it could be me or it could be anybody. No matter what's in the past, or what's happened, everybody needs somebody. She's got so much bottled up inside her. It's like her marriage with Dad; she always says it was the money that was the trouble. But it wasn't. It would help her a lot if she could dig down and get it all out. But she won't.

In a funny way I feel responsible for my mother because I know how lonely she is. It's easier for me now, now that the kids are older. I have them to talk to. It gives you courage to have someone to talk to, to help you. Sometimes Tony will bring Lisa over in the evening and we'll play games or watch something special on TV; most of the time we just sit and talk. It's nice to have someone to help, even if it's just deciding whether we should have roast beef tonight. I'm not a loner. I don't like to make decisions by myself, even on little things.

I was always so scared when my marriages broke up. All that responsibility. I'd sit and look at myself in the mirror and say, "It's all yours now. What are you going to do? Can you do it? What will happen to the kids? What will you do with your life?"

But like now, I'm thinking about opening a dress shop. I thought about having a dress store lots of times, but I never did anything about it. And I'm not the type to dream, just to get down and work hard. I mean, I like to dream but never to take a chance. Years and years ago I wanted to sell real estate and get a license. But I was afraid to because it was a gamble. You live on commission and lose a paycheck. That's the way Mom was too. It's hard to give up security. And Mom saw a lot of businesses go under during the Depression. Security is a hard habit to break.

But I think it was something else too. I think I was afraid to do anything on my own because it was like saying, "I'm through with men. I'm going to be independent." Like saying, "I'm going to be alone for the rest of my life." That's a terrible thing to say when you're twenty-eight or thirty. It's terrible to think you're going to be alone the rest of your life. That step of going into business for yourself seems so drastic, putting you in the category of head of the household and, therefore, eliminating any future. That's the way I always thought about it. It's funny what a few years can do to you, how they change your outlook on life.

When I was single before, I think that underneath I was looking for a husband, wanting and needing one, needing the security of a husband. Now I'm not doing that. I've made it myself all these years and I have enough trust in myself that I can go on. It's like all of a sudden I grew up. Now I think that I can do something if I want to, if I've got enough gumption. Back then, I didn't want to be that secure in myself. I was afraid that if I was, then nobody would want me. It's really funny how you change so much.

When your life gets messed up you lose your confidence. But this time I'm not going to lose it. I'm going to keep it. I've just got to. Because I found out that you can keep it as easily as lose it. I just wish I'd had my confidence a long time ago. And I hope some of it will rub off on the kids. Like I think Lisa stands up for herself more than I did. She's stronger than I was at her age. Now I'm more content within myself than I ever was. Because I've accepted myself for what I am.

Lisa

William Lambertson — Eleanor Ogden

Earl Barlow — Hannah   Nicholas

Ernest Hochman — May   Charles

Norm Peterson — Paul Owens — Grace   Annabel   Irene   Margaret

Bill   Frances

Barbara — Ed Lucas   Carl Eccles — Roger Hirst

Tony Dortch — Lisa   Felicia   Jenny   Ian

Susan

Lisa

Lisa is fifth in the generations of Lambertson women, the last old enough to have a story to tell. She was born in 1953, so it is not a very long story. Like Barbara, like Grace, May and Hannah, she married young—at eighteen—and her daughter Susan, the sixth Lambertson generation, was born in 1973.

Lisa grew up in the 1960s, but her adolescence has a quality of innocence that seems more appropriate to our notions of the 1950s. In what she recalls as her best years Lisa was involved in the intricacies of flirtations and friendships, going steady, winning acceptance by her school's most exclusive group of girls, going to football games, looking forward to the first sign of adulthood, which would come with the ownership of a car. Even her language sounds oddly old-fashioned, as when she talks about sex in terms of going "all the way." The ideas and events of her time—assassinations, the civil rights movement, the Vietnam War, the peace movement—all were distant echoes, none penetrating very deeply into life in the Yakima valley. Of them she may say, "I'm not really into politics," or, "You don't really know the two sides of it." Like others in her family, she defers judgment to higher authority. The people who are running things, she hopes—despite the revelations of Watergate—know what is best.

Her public school years are so recent, and the experience of them so important, that she still places events in time by a reference to the number of her grade; and she keeps mementoes from that time of her life in three scrapbooks: a piece of red cloth on which Tony, the boy she married, once sewed the initials T and L; a wrapper from a Hershey bar he gave her when they were both in eighth grade; clippings from the school newspaper; football programs; napkins and matchbooks from restaurants. Everything is saved so that she will always be able to trace the logical progression of her life.

Her life has brought her to a two-bedroom house in Tacoma, which is a reflection of her entrance into the community of responsible adults. Here are no makeshift wooden crates, odd chairs bought in junk shops, pillows on the floor or any artifacts of youth culture. The living room floor is wall-to-wall sculpted orange carpet; a couch of orange, tan and brown plaid, a club chair upholstered in the same material, end tables and lamps—all have been chosen to carry out a coordinated scheme. When Lisa talks about the future, it is about things that will make domestic life more comfortable: soon she and Tony will be able to afford a washer-dryer; a little later on, she hopes, they will be able to buy an organ and, eventually, a bigger house. Beyond that, she hopes that Tony, who has no special skills or training, will be able to find a job he likes when he gets out of the Air Force; and that she, herself, will be able to finish her vocational training as a dressmaker. She would like to travel a little; they have already been to Disneyland, and she would like to see Yellowstone Park and maybe even Disneyworld, in Florida.

Of the history of the Lambertsons, Lisa knew practically nothing except for her mother's, of which she of course knew a great deal. "Mom's had kind of a messed-up life," she says, and she hopes she has learned not to "take as much guff" from men as Barbara did.

Lisa's world is sparsely peopled. Her friends from Yakima have scattered, and she has not made new ones in Tacoma. Her daily life is bound up with her family's, and her path leads between her own house and her mother's, to the shopping mall and the laundromat, to an occasional movie. At the age of twenty-one, Lisa is, in her own view, a woman settled, the large questions of life already answered. If she is luckier than the other Lambertson women, her future will contain no surprises; it is mapped out, waiting only to be filled in with details.

Lisa: 1953-1974

Pictures bring back a little memory of my dad. It's so weird. I really don't remember him living with us. I remember the house we lived in in Tacoma. Huge. Once Mom had a Tupperware party at that house. So many cars came! And I remember the people who lived next door—Jack and Sylvia. But I don't really remember my dad. Only in pictures that were taken on my birthday, or on Christmas, and I see my dad's in the pictures, so he must have been with us.

My dad tells me that one time I was riding my new bike with training wheels and these kids blocked the path, and I just left my bike and ran home and bawled. So Dad was there then. But once, I remember, I was getting ready for school and I was watching J. P. Patches on TV—he's the guy dressed up like a clown; I still watch him sometimes—and we found out someone had poisoned our cat. I know Dad wasn't living with us then. And another time I was tagging along with the boys next door. They were throwing rocks, and I got hit on the head. Kenny took me over to Mom and she got into hysterics because I was bloody. I don't think Dad was there then. I only remember once when he came to visit and he gave us some toys made out of clay.

What I really remember is when we started going over to Yakima for weekends. Mom must have started liking Carl Eccles. He was an old boyfriend, or something, and we started staying at his grandmother's. But Dad—we didn't hardly see him after we moved to Yakima. He's not the type of person to write. He would send us Christmas gifts once in a while, but then he stopped that. When he got married to

Sherry, that's when he started asking us to come, and we'd see him more at Christmas, or in the summer for a couple of weeks. I was the one who always wanted to see him. I think now that it must have hurt Mom's feelings. I guess she thought I didn't really care for her.

I guess Mom wasn't married to Carl Eccles very long. I didn't like him very well. I remember how he treated his kids, especially the older one, David. Mom says he beat them with his belt. With me and Felicia he didn't use his belt, but when we'd sit at the table, if we didn't like something, we'd have to eat it—even if we'd throw up right at the table. I remember once he was baby-sitting for us and he was making some kind of salad that I didn't like because I don't like tomatoes. He made me go up to my bedroom and stay there. He was very powerful. He had to be the big *man*. To me he was kind of ugly. He was big, and he combed his hair back. He had a big face.

But maybe kids just remember the bad things. I think we had good times when Mom was married to him. We went camping a lot—him and my mom and Grandma Grace. We'd go up in the mountains and stuff. You go back there and there's old mines and stuff. You can see little places where someone's homesteaded. We fished a lot. I'm sure we had a lot of fun. We have movies of when we went camping, and Mom's as pregnant as can be. I don't remember it except for the movies, but I remember when Jenny was born. It was a Friday the thirteenth. Grandma Grace came and stayed with us and when we got home from school we found out we had a sister. Everybody was happy and stuff.

We lived out on the border of Yakima then, and we had acreage and stuff. There was a huge yard all around the house. The neighbors had cows and sheep, and our house had a basement and we were always down there playing, so it wasn't like we were always unhappy. I only remember little things. Like why would it stick in my mind that he sent me to bed because I wouldn't eat tomatoes. I was in the sixth grade when him and Mom separated. I'm sure I was probably relieved.

After that we moved in closer to the city. We had baby-sitters a lot. Really, we had a lot of fun when Mom went out on weekends, because you can do almost anything you want with a baby-sitter. But in those days we sort of thought it was terrible that our mom was going out. Once, I remember, Jenny cut her chin and I had to call Mom at this tavern—the Calico Cat, I think it was—where she went for drinks with people she worked with.

When I was in the seventh grade there was this Joe guy from Seattle Mom was going out with. We liked him. His family had big ranches out here, and we'd go places with his family. And then there was another guy; he had different cars all the time because he worked for this car place. We'd be playing outside, and he'd come driving up in a convertible, or some other kind of car, and the kids would say, "Oh, who's at you guys' house?" And we'd all run over to see. When Mom went out with guys I guess I thought maybe we'd get a new dad.

The years I really remember, it was always Felicia, Jenny, Mom and me. You get to kind of like it. You get to like being on your own. But I felt like I had too much to do. I was only about eleven, but I was the oldest and I had to baby-sit. Even if I just

Lisa:
1953–1974

287

wanted to go to the park across from the house, I had to take Jenny. And here you are going to meet your girl friends, and you've got this little kid with you! Sometimes I'd get sick of Mom going out all the time. I'd get to feel like a drudge. Me and Felicia, it seems like we had to do everything around the house when we got old enough. I would have to clean the living room, vacuum, dust, make the beds, whatever. Felicia'd do the dishes. We'd always goof around until the last minute, and then we'd do everything just before Mom got home, or we'd get in trouble. And if we were going to have meat loaf, it took longer. I remember making a lot of meat loaves. I always hated to do them because they're so cold when you mix them up.

We never had a real homey deal like some people. That's what I might have missed. All my girl friends kind of envied me because we were always doing things ourselves. Now it seems like all their parents are divorced, too. It just took them longer.

I had a hard time when I first started school in Yakima. The school was sort of ahead of the one in Tacoma. They were already learning to write in the third grade, and I had to stay in at recess and practice because I couldn't write yet. I think they were ahead in math too. But after I caught up, school was fun. I liked crafts best. I dreaded history, and math also. But what I remember about school mostly is girl friends and boyfriends. In grade school that was just silliness, where the boys don't really like the girls. Sally Robinson was my best friend, and it was fun to have a real best friend you could tell everything to. When we were in sixth grade, me and Sally would go to her house and listen to records and talk about how when we got out of high school we'd get jobs and get an apartment together and be on our own. We might have done it except she liked somebody too and got married.

I was in sixth grade when they announced over the intercom about how Kennedy was killed. The teacher broke down and everything, and we watched all this stuff about it on television. It was sad. But really, you don't know anything about politics. All you know is that you have a president. Like it was sad when Nixon resigned. It's sad, that's how I feel. A lot of people wanted him to get the whole deal, like even to go to prison. But to me, it's too bad the whole thing had to happen. Like with—who was the vice president who had to resign? Agnew. It's too bad they had to bring all that out. I guess it's good you find out those things, but it's too bad. With Nixon I was just afraid the other countries would think that we were all messed up, that we didn't really have someone running us. That's what really bothered me, not that I thought Nixon was so cruddy. You just wish your head guys wouldn't be messing around like that. They're the people you hope and trust to run the country. But I really felt sorry for him and stuff. We watched a little of the hearings on television, just the part with Dean. But they went on so long. I'm not really into politics.

Junior high was my best years. Maybe because you're just starting to get your nylons, flirting and all that teen-age stuff. I started shaving my legs the sixth-grade summer. Then, when you start the seventh grade, you kind of start watching the styles, and you're trying new makeups. You have boy-girl parties and slumber parties. When I was with girls I knew, I was just fine. But with boys, and people I didn't know, I was kind of quiet. In seventh grade, I remember, I was just wild. My girl friend Belinda Rush, me and her were really close and we were loudmouths, always kidding around in homeroom. But to me, I feel like I'm shy. I liked everybody in school, and I talked to everybody; I had my own little group of friends. But there's one group everybody envied—those girls who would be the cheerleaders. They were usually rich and they had more clothes. Everybody envied those girls. You watch everything they do. They get the cuter boyfriends and everything. I didn't get to be part of that group until I was in eighth grade, and then it was because of a boyfriend.

There's a group of boys who like those girls, and this boy from their group, Stuart Lawson, he started liking me. And, so then, those girls took the time to at least talk to me. Before, it was like I wasn't good enough for them.

Sheila and Diana lived next door to each other and they were pretty high up. You couldn't get in with that class of people unless they liked you. I mean, they won't really associate with anybody lower. But really, once they get to know you, they do. Sheila gave this boy-girl party. No one was in a couple situation except me and Stuart Lawson. It was so stupid. You don't know how to act. The girls were on one side of the room, the boys were on the other. And everybody was throwing candy instead of talking to each other. But then those girls got to know me and they were my best friends. I never got to be a cheerleader, but I always went to games.

I didn't date Stuart Lawson very long. I started dating Tony in eighth grade. He was in my class. I just didn't pay any attention to him until once we were standing around after lunch and Tony's friend, Vincent Curtis, came over to me and said, "Tony wants to talk to you." I said, "What for?" After that Tony started walking me to

291

classes. I think for our first date he asked me to come to the Spring Festival—he was a drummer in the school band. I went by myself and then he walked me home. And that was it. It seems like we always went together. Sometimes, in the summers, we'd break up. I'd like someone else or he'd like someone else. But we'd always end up together.

I never went steady except with Tony and with Vincent Curtis. With Vincent, that was a weird situation. I think it only lasted a week. Vincent started liking me and walking me to classes and stuff. He's a fast talker and, like, I was going steady with him the next day. It's so dumb. He said, "You wanna go with me?" And you're so kiddish, you say, "Oh cool." So he gave me his ring. I was really doing it out of spite because Tony and I weren't going together that summer, and he was ignoring me when we got into the ninth grade. So I thought, "Too bad on you" and started going with Vincent.

Then what happened was, there was going to be a party one Friday, and Tony asked Belinda Rush to go with him. He wasn't really going with her—he didn't ever give her a ring—but he told me later that he wanted to get a girl friend because he was jealous about me and Vincent. So a few days before the party, me and Belinda were standing around with the girls after lunch, and the boys were in their little group, talking and laughing and being stupid. And this other kid, Jackie Curtis, Vincent's brother, comes over to me and says, "Vincent wants his ring back." I said, "Okay" and gave it back. Then Jackie says to Belinda "Oh yeah, Belinda, Tony doesn't want to see you." And the same night Tony called and asked me to go to the party with him. And Vincent started liking Belinda. That was their little scheme.

After that party I remember Tony's and my favorite song was "Poor Side of

Town." Johnny Rivers used to sing it. It was about a rich guy who used a girl, and then he tossed her out. It didn't really relate to us, but it was like Vincent and me breaking up, and how me and Tony are trying to get out of the poor side of town and really belong together. Or something like that.

All the records we ever liked were the love songs. Where maybe a guy lost a girl or the other way around. We listened to rock music, to the Beatles and stuff, but it seems like that's what all those songs were about. I know that people say rock changed their lives and things, but it didn't for me. It didn't stop and make me think or anything.

It was fun to have a boyfriend. Not everyone did. You're at the age when you're just starting with boys, and you're one of the couples. You don't really do much, you're too young. Tony gave me a ring, a letter ring, and he'd walk me to classes and home. After school he had baseball practice, and once in a while I'd go down with a girl friend and watch him. But most of the time I had to go home and do the housecleaning. In between football and baseball seasons he'd come over to the house in the afternoon. Sometimes we'd go over to the park. Or if we were going to a CYO party, his parents would take us there and they'd bring us home. You could hold hands, a kiss here and there. But no big thing. But it's different when you get to high school. Then you have a car.

Roger started coming around when I was at the end of eighth grade. I liked him at first. He'd bring his daughters over once in a while and him and Mom would take us places. We went skidooing once with them and his friend, and we went to church on Sunday. One day him and Mom got home from some where and they said, "How'd you guys like it if we got married?" Afterwards I didn't like him too much. That was the trouble with me and Mom.

Roger's the kind of guy, everybody likes him. Outgoing. Nice. He can make friends. He was nice to us, and we liked him at first. But I had the upstairs bedroom, and I heard all this stuff that went on between Mom and him. Once I heard Mom talking to somebody on the phone. She was crying, saying that Roger had got mad and hit her in front of all these people while they were dancing or something. Called her a slut or a bitch or something. Another time Mom and Roger got into a fight. They went to bed and started talking and got into a worse fight. Mom ended up leaving the house. It was snowing out that night. I don't know where she went; she came back about an hour later.

Felicia never knew about all this stuff. I never told her. Felicia and I didn't get on very well. We were so far apart, four years apart. I'd start talking to her about something, and she wouldn't answer me. I wondered why she clammed up all the time. Later, when we were older, she said she always resented me because I had a boyfriend all the time. When I was practicing to learn to drive, I could see how that would bug her. To her it seemed like I was getting privileges, but really, it was because I had to do more stuff because I was the oldest. So, at the time, Felicia didn't know anything about how Mom and Roger were getting along. I guess she liked him.

I didn't know why Mom and Roger decided to go to Alaska. They weren't married very long then, just a few months, I think. I had one month left of ninth grade, and I wanted to stay and graduate. It was going to be neat, with a dance afterwards and the whole ceremony. Mom said I could stay with my girl friend and her family and then me and Felicia and Jenny would come up to Alaska when school was over. But then me and Mom had a fight about something really stupid—like me being sassy or something—and Roger got mad. He said I couldn't stay, I had to go with them; I guess he thought that would be a good punishment for me. I really resented Mom for that. Before Roger was with her, I'm sure I talked back to her and had teen-age deals like that. But once Roger was with her, that's when we *really* didn't get along. I couldn't see why Mom wouldn't try and change his mind. Felicia and Jenny got to stay in Yakima till the end of the term, and she knew how much I wanted to stay and graduate. But she wouldn't stick up for me. If Roger said I had to do something, I had to do it.

We'd only been up in Anchorage a month when Mom and Roger had that fight. Roger was working in a tavern at night, and he was home during the day, so he'd go to pick Mom up at the bank where she worked. That time I was sitting in the living room, writing a letter to one of my girl friends, and you could tell Mom and Roger'd been arguing when they got home. Mom says to me, "How'd you like to go back to Yakima?" Really, I'd *love* it, but I didn't say that; I just said, "I don't care." Then they told me to go to my room and that's when it started. I heard cups falling, and I came back out. Roger was banging Mom's head against the wall. He was hysterical. They both yelled at me, "Get back in your room!" How was I supposed to stay in my room?

He threw Mom on the floor and I got in the way, so he threw me on the floor and yanked half my hair out. Later, when we were driving back to Yakima, my hair was falling out.

We packed up everything in a hurry that night. I was scared of him and I was scared for Mom. I'll never forget how we packed everything into the car and Roger was on his knees looking out the window from the couch upstairs. He was just laughing at us. I guess he didn't think we were going to make it.

It took us about five days to drive up to Alaska; when we drove back, we did it in three days. Just drove all the time and slept in the car. Mom said she was through with him, that she wasn't going to go back and live with him. I was so relieved.

Then, I don't know what happened, why she changed her mind. He must have talked her into it, I guess. She just said she was going to drive back to Alaska by herself, and us kids would fly up later. I thought I was going to die, thinking of going up there and seeing him again. Mom didn't even talk to me about it or anything. She should have known how I would feel. I always resent her for that. But she's not stupid; if she wanted to live with him that way, I couldn't say anything. When we got off the plane, Roger and Mom met us, and he acted just like always, nice and friendly, like nothing had happened.

When I went to Alaska I wanted to break up with Tony. I felt stupid—us going together when I was up there. I thought he should date and I should date. But he didn't like the idea that I wouldn't be his up there, I guess, and he said he didn't want to. But he ended up wanting to break up four months later. He wrote me this letter and said what I said—that we should date other people. I was broken up about it, but I knew it was better. He didn't say it would be forever, and he said he would write. See, we were both going to high school by then and it's something different from going to junior high. He was at the age where he could get a car and stuff, and you're driving and you mess around with the guys. He had a friend who was older. It's a lot different in high school.

I went out with this guy Charlie up in Alaska. He was older, and we went out to beer parties, stuff like that, which you don't do in junior high. The guys who are old enough buy a six-pack, or whatever, and you'd just drink while you're driving around. I enjoyed it up there. It's different. Like the weather is so different. I even rode a horse in the winter; they put horseshoes on them that are made with spikes. They have snowmobiles and I tried skiing. It was outdoorsy. Once, when I was driving the pickup I almost ran into a moose. And when the sun hardly comes up, well, that's something new to experience. But I wouldn't want to live up there. You feel so isolated from the U.S. You feel like you're living in Europe or something. Up in Alaska people say, "Have you been outside?" Down in the States is what they mean. A lot of people had lived there all their lives. And others were from so many different cities and states. I was really glad when Mom and Roger split up again and we came back down to Yakima.

I didn't have to tell Tony we were coming back, because we weren't going

Lisa:

1953-1974

297

together. But he'd been writing pretty regularly for a while, and he'd sent me a ring. An amethyst, which is my birthstone. So I sent him a postcard saying we were coming.

We got back to Yakima about three in the morning, so we slept in later. And what Tony had done—the night before he got in his car and drove back and forth between Grandma Grace's and Doreen's, because he didn't know where we'd be staying. So that morning my hair was in rollers and the girls came upstairs and said, "Tony's here." I couldn't believe it! He just came driving up. I didn't even know he had a car. He just said, "Can you go and have a soda?" and we just started going together again.

You couldn't ever say me and Tony ever had complete intercourse or something. We were together, but it was kid stuff. There was a lot of feeling each other and stuff like that, but it wasn't all the way. We didn't because I didn't want to have a kid. I didn't want to hurt Mom's feelings.

I don't think Mom ever told me anything. In sixth grade they showed you two films, so you knew about sex. And that was that. I started my period in seventh grade, and I told Mom so she'd get me Kotex. But I don't think I ever talked to Mom about sex, like about how you have a kid. In junior high kids might talk about how parents mess around, because that's how *we* got here. But you don't really think about it. Not your *mom*.

Oh sure, I knew about birth control. But it's just that you don't— Like my girl friends went to Planned Parenthood once, but they told the people there they were

Lisa & Tony

married. They were embarrassed to say they were single. As if you're saying you're messing around all the time. It's the idea of people thinking you must have intercourse every day. I suppose Tony could have used something, but he was probably embarrassed to go into a drugstore. I guess we never did go all the way, because we knew we loved each other and we knew it could wait. There's always that thing of wanting to try it, but there's your subconscious, or something, where you just don't.

Tony didn't worry much about the war. They only drew names for the draft twice, and Tony got high numbers both times. So he was kind of riding it. When you're younger, it doesn't bother you about the war. You don't really think that there's fighting going on unless maybe you have a girl friend whose brother gets killed. But as you get older, the guys you know are starting to go in the Army and they start to talk about it. They talked about it in school too. At history class, and in my humanities class. That was such a different kind of class—we just got to say whatever we wanted. Kids would talk about how they felt about those guys who were running away to Canada, stuff like that. To me, I felt you shouldn't have to join something you really don't believe in. But, really, we didn't know everything that was going on.

My dad, he's very much against that, because he's American and he thinks everyone should join the service. He was in the Navy, in the Korean War, I guess. And I guess half those guys might just have been running to Canada and they don't even stop to think about what they believe.

The thing you thought about when you heard about demonstrations or massacres or things like that—like when they killed those kids at that Kent State college—you don't really think about *why*. You just think it's terrible they killed someone. Because you're a kid like them, you think it's wrong they killed them.

Really, you don't know the inside of it that much. Like I didn't read the paper. But once we saw this movie. It was about these kids, a couple, that took over an office in a college because they wanted to get a point across and the older people wouldn't listen to them. They'd say, "Sure, we'll talk to you," and then they wouldn't even sit down and talk to them because they're kids. So the only way they figured they could get their point across was to demonstrate and take over. So they took this office over, and all the kids got in a circle and they were singing some song that had to do with it. And these guys came in with tear gas and clubs and things like that. The kids were all sitting there and they weren't going to move, so the guys were clubbing them, and kids were being thrown all over the place and there was blood all over. I think it's just too bad, so terrible it had to end up like that, that the generations couldn't sit down and really talk about it. Like with Kent State. It shouldn't really have gotten that far.

The thing is, I never really read the papers or knew the background of the two sides. I don't believe in breaking windows and really rioting; like in that movie—I didn't really believe they should have taken over the school. Some of the kids are wilder and started banging things up and wrecking them. If they had taken over the office, it should have been more controlled—which it couldn't have been because it was too large of a group. But that was the only way they seemed to be able to get what they wanted. Except for the end. They didn't get anything in the end. They just got clobbered.

Nothing like that ever happened in Yakima. No demonstrations or anything.

Lisa:
1953-1974

Once, though, there was this one little drive-in that all the kids would go to. Kids would park there and talk and get something to eat; it was a hangout for the kids. There were a bunch of kids there from different schools, and I guess it was getting out of hand. So the owners called the police. It got kind of messy. No one was hurt, but the kids threw rocks and stuff at the police. That's the only thing like that that ever happened. It didn't have anything to do with the war. It didn't have to do with drugs either.

There *were* drugs around Yakima. You thought you knew the kids who were taking drugs; they seemed different. I've smoked marijuana, but I never took anything hard. I know there was LSD, and whatever, but I didn't take it. I guess I was in eleventh grade when I first smoked marijuana. Tony would get one or two lids once in a while, and we'd smoke with a couple of friends. It doesn't turn me on that much.

I don't think me and Tony ever actually talked about getting married. I don't think he ever proposed—just sillywise really. I think the way it worked was that if we were still together when we graduated high school, we might get married. Tony didn't really know what he wanted to do.

Tony's always worked. His first job was selling Watkins Products, which is kind of like Fuller Brush. He did that when he was little. Then he started as a dishwasher at Sambo's Restaurant—that was when he was in ninth grade. Sambo's is a chain on the West Coast; they're open twenty-four hours a day and mostly they specialize in breakfasts—pancakes and stuff, like the story of Little Black Sambo. They have lunches and dinners and stuff. It's a pretty nice place. It's supposed to be a family restaurant.

The way you work your way up in Sambo's is if you're a dishwasher, you practice with the cooks. You just gradually learn to cook. You have to be fast. Gosh, they flip those pancakes so fast. And the eggs. Tony was working as a cook before we got out of high school.

Tony finished high school in Yakima, but Mom and us moved over to near Tacoma before I graduated. It was because of Roger being in that hospital. At that point I wasn't talking to Mom anymore. I told her over and over: "It's Roger. I don't want to live with Roger." She wouldn't understand, so I would just sit there and say yes or no when she talked to me.

He was always putting Mom down, from the very beginning, it seemed like. Now Mom isn't that much of a homebody, where she'll get up and clean the house. To tell you the truth, I've never seen her get with it and clean the whole house. Usually me or Felicia does it. Roger wanted *her* to do it. He would just blow up at her, always put her down for stupid things. I thought Mom was stupid to live with him. Especially after he was arrested.

One night he called us from the hospital, and we were supposed to get on the phone and say hi to him. I was doing homework and I said, "I'm not saying hi to *that* guy." Oh, Mom was madder than heck. I was bawling and she hit me. But I didn't say hi.

Mom just couldn't understand that I was not going to live with that bastard even if I had to die. Or she didn't want to understand. He just made me sick. No one understood, really. Even the grandmas thought I was just being rebellious. They

303

backed Mom up. I know Grandma Grace liked Roger. Everybody liked him. Even Felicia and my cousins got on my back because I hated him so.

Things would have been fine if Mom had let me go live with my dad, but she didn't want to. She even got Tony to come over and try to talk me out of it, but I wouldn't even talk to Tony. One day I said, "If you're not going to let me live with Dad, I'm not living here anymore. Just go ahead and send me to Remann Hall." Which is a reformatory. Mom said she was going to call Remann Hall. She went to the telephone, but she called Dad and Sherry instead and went over to talk to them. And then Dad came over that night and got my stuff. I guess they talked her into it. Ugh. It was terrible. Those were my worst years. Mom even read my diary, and the reason she thought I was being so rebellious and hateful is that I had put in my diary that I smoked marijuana. If I were her, I would have felt pretty put down. That's not very nice—to read my diary. I think Mom feels pretty bad about it now. She went through all that with Roger, and she ends up divorcing him anyway. I don't know what I would have done without Tony in those years. I think he saved me; if I didn't have him, I think I would have had an emotional breakdown.

It was okay living at my dad's, but they have three other kids and it was just so different from living with Mom and my sisters. I felt like the outcast of the family. Sherry really cares for me and Felicia like we were her own daughters, but it was still different. I didn't talk to Mom until just before Christmas. She invited me over and I went, and then I moved back with her about two months before school was over. By that time Tony and I decided to get married.

• • •

I had all the required courses to finish high school, and I was taking trade sewing at vocational school. I liked it. I like doing something with my hands. I had sewed for myself in high school. I made all my own clothes, and I wanted to finish voc school. But when we decided to get married, that seemed more important.

At first we were going to wait for a year, but we decided—what for? Tony had a job at Sambo's and everything, and a year seemed like such a long engagement. It seemed like we were engaged from when he had given me a promise ring, a couple of years before. That's not really an engagement ring; it's sort of an engaged to be engaged ring. But I always liked it, and we figured we probably would get married unless something happened. But we didn't decide until Tony just called me up one night after I'd left Dad's and he said, "Why don't you tell your mom?" That's when we set the date. We told Mom it would be August twenty-first.

I started making my dress at voc school. Usually at school we did other people's hems and alterations and stuff. But it was always for older ladies, and they're bulging here and there, so you have all these different sizing deals you have to do with the pattern. I guess they had to pay the school, but it was real cheap. I learned a lot, but those women don't spend that much on material, and they'd bring a size-ten pattern, when they were really size fourteen or sixteen. So it was really nice making my own dress.

It only took me two weeks to make it. They have really huge tables to cut out patterns, and we used power machines, the kind they have in factories. They're twice as fast as a regular machine.

My dress was white, with three tiers, gathered. It had an empire bodice, lace sleeves with a puff, and pointed. A square neck. I made the veil out of the real small netting, and the slip underneath of a stiffer kind. I made Felicia's dress and all the other bridesmaid dresses. They were just like mine, except they didn't have the long sleeves and they were different colors. Felicia's was green and Jenny had blue and Mom's was blue and white.

We had the bridesmaids' deal about a week before the wedding—where you make them some cake deals. I'd gotten different colors of the netting in the colors of the girls' dresses. You put the cake in foil, and in netting, with little bows, and you hand it out like a souvenir. And I gave them all a necklace. Tony's sister, Vivian, was a bridesmaid, and Meg, who was at voc school with me. I had always thought that when I got married Sally Robinson would be a bridesmaid for me. But it was too hard for her to get over here to try the dress on, and it was the same with me for her wedding.

We had the rehearsal the night before the wedding, and Dad paid for dinners for everybody at some buffet place. And then the next day, right before the ceremony, we were in the room, getting dressed, and I start crying, and Mom starts crying. And people are saying, "Now, don't *do* this!" But you know, *everything's* going through your mind. I was so nervous to walk in front of all those people; I was afraid I might fall down. And it's exciting, because you've never been married and you know there's responsibilities too. You know you have to start cooking and cleaning for someone. At least, though, you're doing it for yourself and someone you love. So it seems like it'll be fun. And you've gotten away from grown-ups, and you're on your own. Really, you don't know what it's going to be like. You can't imagine.

The wedding was at a Lutheran church outside Tacoma. Little Grandma and

Jenny, Lisa, & Felicia

Lisa

Lisa & Felicia

Lisa & Tony

Lisa & Tony
after their wedding

Grandma McCormack and relatives from my dad's side and Tony's side. We had one reception at the church, and then we had a reception at Jack and Sylvia's for people who wanted to drink and stuff.

We didn't really know where we were going to go for a honeymoon. We thought we'd go to Canada, but we didn't know *where* to go in Canada. Neither of us had been to the Portland zoo, so we got Tony's dad's car, and we went that way. It started raining as soon as we got in the car. The first night we stayed in a motel in Olympia, and the next day we got to Portland. They had a big science pavilion, it takes you all day to go through that deal. They have weird things—like this lamb that was born with two heads, and things to do with the heart and lungs, like of someone who smoked and someone who didn't. They had just everything you could think of about science and inventions. I think we stayed away three or four days altogether. And then we came back. We went to Tony's parents when we got back, because his dad had to cosign so Tony could buy a car. You have to be twenty-one to buy one without a cosigner. We were just eighteen.

We already had our apartment in Yakima. It was a little place, real cute, just off the freeway near the bus depot. We lived there for about eight, nine months. Then we rented a house real far out of town. Tony kept on as a cook at Sambo's. He was going to stay a cook until he found something else. He didn't know what. He thought maybe he'd go to school. I had a job for a while at The House of Fabrics, but I got laid off because they were just putting in the new mall downtown and business went down. And then Tony got asked to be assistant manager at Sambo's. The assistant manager keeps the books and calls to get what they need meatwise. And if somebody can't get the manager, they call the assistant manager—like if somebody quits or something. The manager is there during the day, and Tony had to be there at night. When he was a cook, he only worked eight hours a day. But when he was promoted it got to be about thirteen hours a day. Friday and Saturday nights he had to work from five in the afternoon till five in the morning. And after he'd till up the money, he wouldn't be home until six-thirty. And then he had to go back and work on Sunday afternoon. First he was getting two days off a week, then it was one day, and then it got to be one day every other week. It's really kind of a pushy deal. Tony never got paid extra for working late. They didn't have a union. Tony wanted this medical deal the union had. But the manager talked him out of it because the whole group has to have it and the company has to pay. So the company didn't like that. They just paid for Tony's medical insurance separately.

What we were going to do was get to be managers. It's like a franchise. Being a manager, you get six hundred dollars a month plus twenty percent of what the store makes. That's after you pay off what you owe them, which should take two years in a good-running store. And after you pay them off, you can put money into other stores. And if the manager's wife works, you get three hundred more a month.

So we were going to do that. You have to be twenty-one, but they were going to start training Tony before that. They would place him with managers who were opening new stores, and then he'd have six weeks at some class learning more about the

Lisa & Tony

books. Then they put you in a store as assistant manager until there's an opening someplace you'd like. But we heard from a guy who'd done it that he and his wife were splitting up. He'd married a waitress and they got to be managers, and it just wasn't working out. So we figured it wasn't too good for young couples. It's better if you're in your thirties and your kids are in their teens. Even as it was, we couldn't go anywhere together. Tony's folks had an anniversary dinner, but Tony had to work, so I had to go by myself. His brother, Jay, had a graduation dinner, and I had to come by myself. If we were managers we'd have no family life.

I found out I was pregnant five or six months after we got married. It's not that we wanted a baby desperately. We weren't asking for it. We just never worried about it. I never thought, "Oh I'm going to get pregnant." Just—if I got pregnant, I got pregnant. We never thought about it that much.

When I found out, I didn't tell Mom or anybody. We wanted to keep it a secret as long as we could. But then Tony's brother got the measles and I was worried; I didn't know if I'd had them already, so I called Mom to ask her and she guessed right away. I had morning sickness terribly, so I suspected it even before I got the checkup at the doctor's.

We were pretty happy about it. We worried we wouldn't have enough money, but we wanted kids early. Tony's sister, she's been married five years and they don't have kids. They feel they'd rather live while they're young. They're both working full time. With us, we can have fun with Susan. They might get too old to have fun with their kids.

Lisa:
1953-1974

313

I didn't have time to think about being scared when Susan was born. I went to the doctor, and he said I should have already delivered by then, because I was dilated four inches. So he said to come to the hospital the next day and he would induce it. I was a little nervous, but not really.

I got to the hospital about seven in the morning. Mom was with me. She'd come over for the weekend, and she said she'd stay. What got me more than anything was one of my girl friends from junior high was in the hospital when I got there. She'd been in labor for fourteen hours, and she was screaming and everything. That bugged me; I was thinking, "Oh, shut it!" I wasn't having any pains until they broke the water. Then the doctor gave me a shot for pain. But I was awake when I was delivering Susan. I saw her being born. It's such a neat thing.

See, when I got married, I never looked at the future. I never thought about what it was going to be like. I just thought about now. It was going to be fun—at first, anyway. I suppose you think it'll always be the way it is at first. Well, since we have Susan, it's not bad, but it's not roses. You're not always holding hands, or always together. The romantic goes down, because you're both doing things and you've got your different schedules. One might be tireder than the other, and if you want to go somewhere, the other might say he doesn't feel like it. But still, you grow older too, so it all kind of changes. You're not kids anymore. Having Susan gave us more, responsibilitywise.

After Susan was born I worked at Sambo's as a hostess for a while—for about a

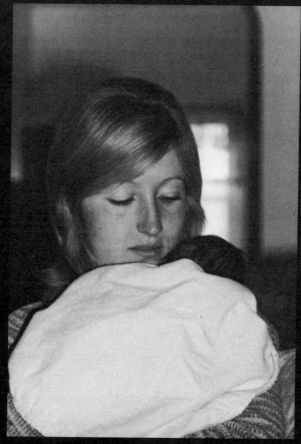

Lisa & Susan: 1972

month and a half. The cook's wife baby-sat Susan. Tony said we'd be working together, but it ended up I'd be working days and he'd be working nights. So I quit, and then all I did was baby-sit Susan or go shopping or go to a girl friend's house. We lived so far out of town, mostly I stayed home. Then, after we decided not to be managers, there wasn't that much opportunity for anything over in Yakima. Tony was getting fed up. He really didn't know what he wanted to do. He didn't want to get into anything else that had to do with food—like McDonald's or other restaurants. And he didn't want a paper job, where he'd have to wear a suit and everything. So he thought maybe he should join the service. He's always liked photography; he had a class in it in high school, and he developed film and everything at home. He heard that the Air Force had a course in photography, and he thought maybe they would send him to school in that. And being in the service, you get a lot of benefits.

The Air Force sent him to Texas for his basic training, and then somewhere else in Texas to school. They trained him in something to do with the loading of planes. It's not what he wanted, but there's a GI plan when you get out and it's a lot cheaper to go to school. Maybe he can get into photography when he gets out. And the benefits help you buy a house. And if we had another kid, it would only cost us forty dollars. Susan cost almost nine hundred dollars. We had to pay off a lot of that before she was born; and after, we didn't have the money, so they let us pay it off in three months. And now we can go to the commisary once every two weeks and spend like thirty-five dollars on food for all of us. That must save us about twenty dollars. And medicalwise, Susan's allergic to something, and we just go in and they give you this medicine free.

Maybe Tony should have gone to college. But really, he doesn't know what he wants to do yet. A little while ago he was talking to his parents, and he said maybe he should have been a doctor. But that takes *so* long. And he doesn't want to be a baby doctor, and he doesn't want to be an operating doctor. When he gets out of the service, he's going to start taking some courses, and maybe he'll find out what he wants to do. He knows he doesn't want to stay in the Air Force. They're so strict about the haircuts. They don't care how long your hair is on top now—it's not crew cuts anymore—but they have to be shaved around the ears. My dad says they have to have discipline; they have to keep the guys in line. But we don't believe it's necessary. They've got to change a little with the times.

And Tony doesn't like having to go to commander's call once a week. And he has to go to so many classes. Like they teach something about lower- and higher-class people. He has to go to so many little meetings all the time. That's something you don't know about when you join. And some other class where they teach about racial deals. About blacks and whites.

I guess it's good to learn about it, but, to me, certain blacks bug me terribly. The ones where their kids grow up with such a bad attitude about us. We don't have such a bad attitude about them where we would call them niggers. There are these little kids who live behind Mom's house; they're just a little older than Ian and Susan, and they're calling us honkies and stuff. It just bugs me. And like Indians. We saw that movie *Billy Jack* the other weekend. Now I heard that we do break a lot of treaties with the Indians, and I do sort of feel sorry for them because we are the most populated. They're not *all* wrong. But over in Yakima, the blacks were much friendlier. Over here they're

Tony
(top row, middle)

so much tougher. They give you the shivers. You're afraid to walk around with them. There's one black woman across the street; her boys are in their teens, and they'll say "hi" to us. I don't care if Susan plays with her. It's just the ones that are so stuck-up. I'll say hi and some'll give you the snub. I was watching some clips on television from Martin Luther King—the one who had all those peace walks. He seemed like someone the blacks needed. Especially the ones who are so religious. He looked so neat. He's someone you could look at. Not like the ones who do that hand deal with their fists, those who don't stop and think about the peaceful side of it. Really, it seems like they're just out to get what they can.

I guess a lot of people are out to get what they can. But right now I'm happy with what we've got. That's what I told Tony. I think he worries—maybe all men do—that he should make more money so he could give more. We're not poor and we're not rich. If we had more money we'd just be spending more and wanting more. Oh sure, I want things. I want to get an organ—one of those new ones with all the things you can push, like drumbeats. A piano seems so plain. We might not be able to get that for another year, because I want my washer-dryer first. If we had enough money we'd just go and buy them, but then we'd be wanting a swimming pool or something else we couldn't have. This way we have things to look forward to, a goal.

I'm always looking at houses. People probably always wish they had a better one. I do want a big house, an older one with pretty much original stuff, like the one Mom almost got in Yakima before we left. With a big dining room, living room with a fireplace, all kinds of little rooms. In a house like that I'd like to have carpeting maybe

Lisa:
1953-1974

319

just in the halls and in the dining room, but in the living room, maybe one of those Persian rugs. And I want to have a room where I could sew.

When I sew I really get into it. Usually when I sit down to make something I can get it done real fast. At voc school we learned to hand sew; you baste and then back stitch. That's how the Paris designers do it. It seems so slow, monotonous, but it's worth it. It looks nicer than machine stitching. I'm a careful sewer, but I can do it so fast. I've learned so many short cuts. I can't do much at home now, because Susan runs around. I have to do it at night, and then I make such a mess. I'd like to sew for two days straight and be able to leave everything set up.

If I'd finished voc school I'd know more. Like I don't really know how to completely make a pattern. And also, having the diploma helps you get a job. The school puts you in your first job. You might get a job tailoring in a store, where you tailor men's jackets or women's formals or whatever they need. My cousin, who's a year younger than me, finished voc school, and they got her two jobs. One is tailoring, which she likes. The other is dry cleaning. So she's got two part-time jobs. If Mom gets that shop, I'd like to work there for a while. And I might like to take interior design. I might be artsy, because that sounds interesting.

I think I will finish voc school because we're only having one kid. I started taking birth control pills after Susan was born. And Mom and I had a garage sale, and we sold all of Susan's and Ian's baby stuff. For somebody who's a homebody, it would be all right to have more, but I think one's enough for me. You're just so tied down. I'm glad we did it this way, because when Susan's finished school, we'll still be young enough to enjoy things. We would like to have a little boy, but you could try three times for that. There's so many goods and bads about having only one kid. But the way money is right now. Maybe if we were rich—but I still think I'd only want one even if we were. I think Susan'll probably be lonelier; maybe that's bad for her. But I could put her in a nursery school, and I'm not going to be away from her all the time. If we want to go on a camping trip, it's easy to take only one kid. And if there are just the three of us, we might be able to afford to go to Hawaii. She'll maybe be more part of the family.

But then sometimes I think that maybe, when you get old, you want more kids to come and see you, and more grandkids. Or maybe Susan'll get killed in an accident. I hate to think about that. I've still got till I'm thirty to think about having another one. I wouldn't want to wait any longer than that. When Mom had Ian, oh, that was too late. I guess it was to save the marriage. I guess in the back of her mind it was her third marriage and she thought she was getting too old for another divorce, trying to start over.

Mom kind of got used by a lot of men, really. I don't know if her feelings were too much in the way. I have feelings, but I know from seeing Mom how it hurts her a lot but it's not getting her anywhere. Not so far, anyway. Each time she did something good for them, or stuck with them, it always ended up bad anyway. I don't honestly know why that happened to her. I don't really know how she acted with my dad, and with Carl Eccles. I didn't watch. She might have been sad all the time. She told us once that she didn't really love my dad when she married him. I don't know why she got married then. Unless to have me. She wanted to hold on all the time. I don't know if it was for us kids or for herself.

I wouldn't stick it through like Mom did with Roger. That would be a divorce for me. When we first got married I said to Tony that I would never get a divorce if we had a kid—for the kid's sake. But now I think that if we absolutely didn't get along, I would. Susan's not stupid. She'd know that's no family life. Maybe that's how I'm different from Mom. I hope. Maybe because of all she's been through I've learned a lesson. I won't take that much guff from a guy. If me and Tony can do things and enjoy each other, that's fine. Like we were out in the yard one day; Tony was shoveling and I was raking. And the next-door neighbor came out and said, "That's what I like to see. You guys working together." But if we get where maybe we can't sit down and talk—or if he beat me excessively, or if he put me down and made a fool of me—I don't like it when the man's too powerful, like in the olden days. To some people the man's the head of the house. But if he was always telling me what to do, if he couldn't get up and fix his own snack once in a while, that'd be too bad. I just couldn't live like that all the time. If he couldn't pick up his own beer bottles and stuff. I don't believe in running after him, telling him to do this or pick up that. But I don't believe in him telling me everything to do.

I suppose if I was real sloppy about the house, he'd probably get on me. Which I can see, because I should clean the house. But I'm not that sloppy. He's never hit me or anything; I know it would be pretty drastic if he did. Unless it was something silly where I deserved it. We might have been drunk and I said something I shouldn't have.

Even if Tony had an affair, if it was a quickie affair, I'm sure we'd still be together. If it was a long one, I'm sure we'd get a divorce. If it just happens once, you can't condemn someone forever. But if it was a week or a month, I'd really think about it. If *I* had an affair, though, especially like a quickie, it seems it would ruin our marriage.

In magazines and stuff, you read how you're dependent on your husband. You don't think about it until you read something like that. Well, in a way I am, because I'm not working or anything. But, see, Tony might have to get transferred to another base for a month, and I don't feel I couldn't live without him. Even if he was transferred to Europe for a year and we couldn't go. I'd probably just get a job.

In a way, though, I guess I am dependent. I don't really have any friends over here. Me and Mom were talking about that. One time she needed some garbage taken out, and she asked some guy if she could borrow his truck. And he never showed up. It hurt her that she didn't have anybody she could count on. Sally Robinson will probably always be my closest friend, but she doesn't live over here. We have a couple we go see in Yakima once in a while, but half my friends from Yakima are in different cities; you don't really know where anymore. And other people, well, it usually happens that Tony'll like the guy and I won't like his wife, or the other way around. I'd like to look up Meg, my friend from voc school, but I don't think Tony would like her husband.

Tony was saying we should go out with somebody from the base. But his days off are so limited that they might have to work when Tony's not working, or you both might have a different hobby. So he hasn't brought anybody home, and maybe he never will. If we do meet someone, it would be maybe if we went to some cocktail place. Or maybe if there was a neighbor, I might have a neighbor friend and we could do things during the day. But then Tony has different shifts, so some days I couldn't see her.

Together, I don't think me and Tony will ever have someone to go out with a lot. There are just *so* many things; you have to find a couple you both get along with and your husbands have the same hours.

Most of the guys at the base are single anyway. We took this one guy up to the mountains one Sunday to have a picnic, but I think he felt stupid being by himself. Tony has some friends and they might go out to drink, but he doesn't want to bring them home. Single guys are different from married guys. If there are just guys, they talk guy talk. You know, women sit down and talk about clothes or shopping. Tony talks about guns and archery and stuff like that.

Right now Tony works from four in the afternoon until twelve. He sleeps until eight, eight-thirty, and we can do things during the day. In the summer we might go to the beach all day and take a lunch. Now we're working on the yard. Or if I have the car I might go shopping or go see Felicia. And we go to shows. I just turned twenty-one, so now we can go out to cocktail places and drink. Before, if we wanted a drink, we'd go to Mom's or Dad's. Last summer we drove to Disneyland with Susan. We were gone nine days, and we camped sometimes and stayed in motels. Mom offered to baby-sit Susan, but it was no bother to take her. She was only nine months old, but she enjoyed it.

We really liked Disneyland. He had such ideas! It was a lot better than just a fair.

We stayed there thirteen hours. And then we looked around Los Angeles and went out to Universal City and toured through that on a bus. Tony gets a month off next year, and I'd like to have another trip. Maybe to Yellowstone. And, eventually, we'd like to go to Disneyworld in Florida.

At night, when Tony's at work, I might go to Mom's or stay home. If I'm home I might read or watch television. I like to read. I like mysteries. When I was young I liked the young mysteries; now I like the older ones. Half the time I have to go all the way through a book to know if I've read it before. I like love stories too. And there was one book I liked by a black author, about himself. I'm terrible about authors' names. I've read *The Learning Tree,* that's a good one.

Sometimes I read a book that really makes me think. Like *Chariots of the Gods.* It says that people from outer space really created all of this. Everything. And they're just kind of watching us. They were here a long time ago, because they found all these things on Easter Island that they left. Books like that make you question about God and religion. But you still believe in God. With all the bad things, you hope that something's good. Sometimes it seems impossible that there is a God, but you have to have something to believe in. And it sounds like a good idea, everything about God they talk about.

These people were talking about Billy Graham's book, and they said that the way the Catholics and Protestants are fighting over there in Ireland, that's supposed to be one of the signs of the world ending. And the Negroes, when they start rioting, that's another sign. Those kinds of things make you stop and think because the Bible was written so long ago and now these things are happening. Sometimes I say, "Looks like

Lisa:
1953-1974

325

the end of the earth's coming, the way everything's going." But I guess I don't take it very seriously. Like they say that Washington's going to have an earthquake. You don't really believe it unless it really does happen.

Sometimes I talk to Felicia about stuff like that. Felicia and me are closer now; we can talk about things more. She's kind of shy at first, like me. But when she gets to know you, she can be funny and stuff. I remember one time we went out for a walk, to get a 7Up or something, and she was saying how, when she got older, she'd get a job and an apartment. She said she'd like to shack up with a boy and share the bills and stuff. That would worry me. Because what if all of a sudden he left you? In marriage you have a contract where you would go to a lawyer and you would split the bills, so you weren't left with everything. I don't think I would ever do that, shack up. I don't know why it would be different from living with a girl friend. I've thought about that. If you're sharing an apartment with a girl friend, you're two different people and you might not get along. But it seems worse if it were a guy.

Tony and I never thought about living together and not getting married. I don't think it's because I'm for the old standards. To me it's all right if Felicia wants to. But if the guy just left, that's the part that would bother me. If he just left.

Once we were talking about birth control stuff when Felicia thought she was going to marry Tony's brother. I said that she shouldn't be stupid and get pregnant to help her and the guy's relationship. Some people might think, well, I'll have a kid and maybe he'll love me more. That's a stupid reason. It's both your faults, but it's stupid on the girl's part if she had that in the back of her mind. I guess I learned that from what Mom's been through. Having kids never helped her. Mom's never been that

326

Lisa, Hannah, & Felicia

Ian, Hannah, & Susan

affectionate with us either. I don't know if it's because she didn't have time when we were little and she was always out working. But I don't think she was even when she wasn't working.

If you have a kid you have to be so careful when you get remarried. You've got to be sure he really cares for your kid. Such a hard situation. And to get remarried, it wouldn't be the same to me lovewise. The first love—of course I've never been in love a second time. I don't know if Mom ever has. Maybe it was just loneliness that made her get married.

With me and Tony, we disagree about a lot of things. He doesn't make me think his way, and I don't make him think my way. We just say our opinions. He'll listen if I talk to him about something, having a problem or feeling bad. He doesn't say, "Oh, that's stupid." But he doesn't say, "Oh, that's too bad" either.

I might say, "Why don't you pick up your clothes more?" But he won't say that he will the next time. I guess he's pretty easy to get along with. He's impossible, sometimes, but I'm sure I'm impossible sometimes. Like if I'm in a mean mood and I don't really listen to him. We used to like to shop together a lot, but now he doesn't like to go and I'd still like him to go. So we've come to an agreement: I usually go by myself. I'd kind of enjoy us going to the mall and looking around at what they've got. But if I've got to get Susan underwear, he doesn't like to go.

We agree about raising Susan. It's been mostly me raising her, but I think he should get in there spankingwise, and he does. We want her to go to college; we're saving for it now. We take out a twenty-five-dollar bond every three months. When she's eighteen, we'll get three or four thousand dollars. We'd be happy if she wants to go to college, but at least something like voc school. If she wants to be an artist, she can go to art school. If she falls in love and wants to get married, there's no way I'm going to stop her. I still hope she'll go to college, but it's up to her.

Sometimes I just wish me and Tony would sit down and talk more. It seems like we get up and always have to do stuff and get ready to go to the laundromat and stuff like that. There always seems to be something that's taking up our time. And then I have to fix dinner, and he's about ready to go. And on weekends you have to run errands and stuff like that. Of course some days we talk too much.

Before you get married you think that it'll be like it is in books and music. Being married, of course, you're not lonely. I would be lonely if I was by myself. But if you had a girl friend, that would help quite a bit. Especially if you're dating. I think Mom's probably lonely. I mean the kids are there, but that's like living with a girl friend. You have to get out and see a guy even if it's only once a month. You need that side of it.

Mom shouldn't think her life is over. She works, she can meet people. She's not bashful or quiet. Grandma Grace, even Grandma McCormack, if they get out maybe they'll meet an old guy whose life is just as lonely. If that happened to me, if Tony died or something, I'd hope I could get out and do things. I wouldn't start a new family or anything like Mom did with Ian. I wouldn't do that for any reason. That's too much responsibility for Mom. I just think she's too tired for that kind of stuff.

I hope I don't have any divorces. It seems to be a tradition in our family. Mom and the grandmas never talked to me about those things. It's something they don't get into. There are a lot of things I didn't know. I didn't know that Little Grandma didn't have a mom. And I didn't know she was married three times. I only remember one of the grandpas. He had a long beard and he was laying in bed in the living room and he was chewing tobacco and he spit it out. I guess that was Mr. Nesbitt. And I never knew any of Grandma McCormack's husbands. Or Grandma Grace's. It's been all grandmas around here. Except for Mom's dad, who died when I was in tenth grade.

I don't see any of the grandmas much. I saw Grandma Grace on Ian's birthday, just a little while ago, over at Mom's. But Tony wouldn't enjoy just going over to see them. I'd have to go myself. I care for Grandma Grace a lot, but you get sort of a kick out of Grandma McCormack. She doesn't seem like Grandma Grace's mother. They both seem the same age to me. Grandma Grace seems like she's sick all the time, and Grandma McCormack gets out and does things a lot more. She's kind of funny. She's got a little police club hanging on her door, and she always used to kid us kids that she was going to hit us with it. It makes me feel bad that I don't see them more.

Especially Little Grandma now that she is older. When we lived in Yakima we'd go see her sometimes on a Sunday. Not as often as I wish we would have. I remember once when me and Tony were in tenth grade we drove over to see her. I had bangs then, and she started teasing me and telling Tony he was going to have to get my hair cut because it was hanging in my eyes. She's just enjoyable. For her age. She's not cranky. She likes to tell old stories, whatever comes to her mind. I really like to listen to her. I wish we could sit down and look at all of her old stuff and listen to her stories. Like when she was here one day, she talked about how this house reminded her of the house she lived in when she was a kid. She called it her mansion. She said it had one of these porches and there were a couple of maids or something. And then Felicia

Lisa:
1953–1974

331

Hannah & Susan: 1973

pointed to her pin, and she talked about where she got it. She just tells little stories, things she thinks about. I feel so sorry for her. When she's with all of us she can't hear, and we all seem to forget about her. She just sits there.

When Susan was seven days old I brought her over to Little Grandma's, and she told me how she'd fed Uncle Charlie from this bottle that had a long tube. She hung the bottle over the bed, and the nipple was attached to this tube. I guess she didn't breast feed either. I didn't. Not because of the idea of it, but if you go somewhere and the kid's hungry, I couldn't do it in front of people. My girl friend Sally will do it in front of just me. Susan sat next to her, staring, and we were trying to explain it to her. It seems kind of an inconvenience. I don't know if it was in the olden days. It seems hard enough just to have to heat their bottles and give them baby food.

I feel like I could be that much closer to Susan, because Mom and I didn't really talk that much. Mom talks much more to Felicia now. I guess she realized she should be closer to her kids. Mom and I had problems, but of course Mom's had kind of a messed-up life. I want me and Susan to just really get together.

You know, you always wonder what it's going to be like to have a kid. When you see it being born, that's the first time you ever think you've created one. One's growing inside you. It's a miracle, like they always said. I remember when Susan was being born the doctor was teasing me. I was sort of passing in and out, but I saw her head coming through. Then the doctor says, "It's a girl!" I felt like I must have been smiling the whole time. They must have thought I was dumb or something.

Epilogue: December, 1975

I have not seen the Lambertsons for more than a year. Barbara and I keep in touch by letter and telephone, Lisa writes occasionally, and Hannah wrote once a week until she no longer could.

On October 7, 1975, Lisa's second child was born. She and Tony—who has now left the Air Force and is working for a restaurant wholesaler—are very pleased about having a boy.

Barbara has given up, at least for now, her plans to open a dress shop. She didn't think, she wrote, that she could stand the strain at this time: Her twelve-year-old daughter, Jenny, has been having emotional difficulties and has seen a psychiatrist several times. Barbara has also had to sell her house, which became too expensive to keep up. She bought a smaller one and last April held a wedding there for her second daughter, Felicia. "Felicia's husband Dale has a good job and is a nice boy," she wrote. "They seem very happy."

Of Grace and May I have had no direct news. Grace alone of the Lambertson women objected to the manuscript of the book. It was "airing dirty linen," she told Barbara, degrading to the family and belittling to her. On Grace's account, I changed all the names. I regret doing so only because I would like, now, to be able to call Hannah by her rightful name.

Sometime on the Sunday night of June 15, 1975, Hannah had a stroke. She was found the following Tuesday afternoon, conscious, lying on the floor of her house. Her son Charlie and his wife Ruby called an ambulance. Hannah was taken to a hospital and from there to a nursing home. Barbara visited her in the nursing home one day and found her, her head down on her food tray, crying, "Get me out of here. Get me out of here." There was nowhere for Hannah to go. Her landlord had rented her house to another tenant, and in any case, she could no longer live alone. She needed a great deal of attention; caring for her was too great a burden for anyone in her family.

Ruby, who lived nearest, saw Hannah most often. She wrote to me: "Mom just don't eat. A spoon of this or that, a half slice of bread or toast, often nothing but a glass of milk or a cup of tea. She has told us many times if we want to kill her we should put her in a nursing home. I think she is trying to starve herself to death." On November 1, Ruby wrote, "Mom is gradually getting weaker. It is difficult for her to talk. Some days she just sits with her eyes nearly shut. There has been snow on the passes and the Chinook is closed for the winter. Mom is so little and thin."

May came and sat at her bedside one day. Hannah, waking from sleep, raised her daughter's hand to her lips and kissed it. Grace refused to visit. "I want to remember her like she was," she told Lisa.

Hannah's letters to me became almost impossible to read as her eyesight deteriorated even more. She could not see the letters she formed, where to place words on the page, or even where the paper ended. Here and there I could make out a phrase. Again and again she wrote about darkness. "This room is so dark. . . . The rooms here are so long and dark. . . . The room is so dark I cannot see."

And: "Oh for a friend to comfort me. . . . How I long to see you. . . . When I was young it was a disgrace to put a parent away. . . . It's terrible to be shut in such a place. . . . Oh to be free."

In late September a letter came written on a paper towel. I could make out only the last line. "So goodbye dear. I sure had a great life for years. So goodbye for the last time." But she tried once more. She asked to be sent a strong magnifying glass. It didn't help and at last her letters stopped. On November 21 she fell into a coma. She died at 4:30 on the afternoon of November 22, 1975.

Hannah once said to me: "Lots of heartbreak in this life. It's an awful test. I call myself Job sometimes, and I'm not giving my God up. When He sees fit to lift this curse I'll be better off. But when that will be, *I* don't know."

When I heard that she was dead I read the Book of Job.

Oh earth cover not thou my blood and let my cry
have no place. . . . Oh that my words were now written!
oh that they were printed in a book! That they were
graven with an iron pen and lead in the rock forever!

Her God never showed himself to Hannah or lifted the curse. Here is her cry. Here are her words written in a book.

Afterword

Comment by the likes of me seems gratuitous after reading the unselfconscious, candid, and at times quite unnerving personal narratives that make up this book. The author has put together these "oral documents," as they sometimes get called, with skill and obvious affection. She knows what these modest and unassuming women have to offer us; she knows the wisdom they have acquired—after much hard living. She knows, too (as her subtitle tells us), how much they have to teach us about ourselves—about our values and customs, our changing social life, and even, more grandly, our history as a nation. These are ordinary, plain, working-class people. They are white American women, who have not by any means had an easy time of it, yet have fought to stay alive, to carve out for themselves what destiny they could, however limited their circumstances. They are not to be turned into anyone's untarnished heroes; they are not, were not proletarian saints, without warts save those imposed from without—society's injustices become a family's limitations. They have been decent and honorable, but also self-centered and self-pitying. They have suffered injustices, but they have not been without envies, rivalries, moments and longer of narrowness. But in the main they come across as women who have been part of what George Eliot referred to as "common life"—with no pejorative intent; on the contrary, considerable admiration.

I suppose this book has to have its contents categorized. I suppose we can't just let these women be. They were fiercely determined to stay alive and affirm themselves as human beings. They tried the best they knew how to make a go of it, to find whatever comfort and satisfaction life had to offer them—not all that much, at times, but not all that little, at other times. Some of us, alas, will want to analyze the "perceptions" of these women, take stock of their "attitudes," find out what bearing their words have on various psychological, sociological, or political theories that try to account for everyone's "behavior." And no doubt there is plenty of "material" here; the preceding pages are rich with what James Agee called "actuality"—unadorned, scarcely prepossessing, but still complicated and not without those ironies and ambiguities of thought and deed which some of us reserve for the well off, the well educated, the rich. There have been, there still are, novelists who have labored long and hard to bring us nearer to daughters like Hannah's. Truth is not stranger than fiction; truth is there, waiting for the novelist to see it, then give it the added life of narrative coherence. And Dorothy Gallagher, without pretense or apologies, has done what many novelists all the time do; she draws upon "real life," but selectively and imaginatively. Out of all she has heard, she gives us these particular portraits; and the result is our increasing sense of "them"—until "we" and "they" merge as fellow human beings.

Perhaps I can best serve the author's witnesses by calling upon one of my own, an Appalachian woman of forty-five who happens to be a preacher's daughter, and a coal miner's wife. She has over the years I have known her spoken vividly, compellingly, of her life, as does Hannah and those younger women in her family. She has also, I believe, spoken for "Hannah's daughters" and for millions like them, when she has, without pretense or immodesty, tried to explain why it is important for people like her to speak out and be heard: "I wanted to be a teacher. I just couldn't finish school. There wasn't the money. I had to go to work. Then I got married; and the kids came, one after the other. But I used to read those books in our school, and there'd be stories about presidents and governors and generals and kings and all kinds of big, important people. I'd read about these people. I'd wish I could live the kind of life they had lived. I'd start to feel sorry for myself. Sometimes I'd lose all respect for myself. I'd think of myself as a kind of third-rate person, who didn't have anything good to say. It's bad enough being poor, and not finishing school; but when you begin to think you're no good, that's the end of the road.

"But my mother won't stand for us to be against ourselves. Since I was little I remember her telling us: don't you bad-mouth yourselves; don't you ever sink to that level. She wanted us to hold our heads high and to let everyone know that we may not be rich, and we may not have a lot of education, but we're not dumb, and we can size up people, and we know what's going on, and we're as smart about how the world goes as anyone else is, and sometimes smarter than a lot of those big-shot people, who don't know what's actually happening in the world, because they have money and they have books, and when you have a lot of both, you can live in your own world, and you can make up all kinds of ideas about what's going on, but you don't really know, because you're off somewhere in a big house, or reading your books. Our teacher was just like my mother. She had all of us in that one-room schoolhouse, and she had to teach six-year-olds and teach twelve-year-olds, and we were all dirt-poor, and not going to get to college, like she had. But we did our best, I can tell you. We tried. We were hungry for learning. And we didn't want to forget what we'd learned. We tried to figure out what life is all about.

"I'm still trying to do that. I'll take a walk, when I have a few minutes off, and

I'll ask myself why God put us here, and what I should be doing that I'm not doing, and what I'm doing that I shouldn't be doing. I only wish I knew more about God's purposes. I pray to Him. I ask Him to smile on us, my children and my husband and my brothers and sisters and their children. I ask Him to spare the men at work: no explosions in the mines. I ask Him to keep us fed and with clothes. But more than anything else I ask Him to whisper a few words to me about how I should live my life, and what I should tell my kids when they ask me why, why, why. You don't have to be a college professor to want to know why the world is the way it is, and why it isn't a better world, where people are nicer to each other, and there's less meanness around. That's what my mother used to tell us—that there's a lot of meanness in the world, and you have to live through the meanness, and prove that you're an alright person, even if you've been a little mean yourself sometime. I will think about what my mother told me and what I tell my kids when I'm off by myself walking. I know there are others all over the world talking to themselves like I do. I wish we could get together, and see each other; or at least get to know what we're all thinking. It helps to have company."

She would be good company for "Hannah's daughters," and they for her. Her struggles, the struggles of the women whom we get to know in this book, are utterly important, and never to be considered in any way less significant or revealing or exemplary than those of men and women who are part of what the Bible refers to as "the powers and principalities," or for that matter, men and women who write books, or whose biographies are written up. All of which may be a bit "defensive"—an unnecessary effort to justify and defend one set of lives at the expense, perhaps, of others. But

342

it is unfortunately still true that for most of us readers women like those we have just met in the preceding pages are all too unfamiliar—their lives, their small triumphs and grave moments of sadness or despair, their earnest and unceasing attempt to make do, to persist, to keep going, keep going, whatever the unyielding, concrete social and economic obstacles, or the sudden, unpredictable assaults sent by fate.

Robert Coles, M.D.